Hands-On Data Structures and Algorithms with Kotlin

Level up your programming skills by understanding how Kotlin's data structure works

Chandra Sekhar Nayak
Rivu Chakraborty

BIRMINGHAM - MUMBAI

Hands-On Data Structures and Algorithms with Kotlin

Commissioning Editor: Richa Tripathi
Acquisition Editor: Shriram Shekhar
Content Development Editor: Tiksha Sarang
Technical Editor: Mayank Dubey
Copy Editor: Safis Editing
Project Coordinator: Prajakta Naik
Proofreader: Safis Editing
Indexer: Mariammal Chettiyar
Graphics: Jisha Chirayil
Production Coordinator: Tom Scaria

First published: February 2019

Production reference: 1260219

Published by Packt Publishing Ltd.
Livery Place
35 Livery Street
Birmingham
B3 2PB, UK.

ISBN 978-1-78899-401-9

www.packtpub.com

`mapt.io`

Mapt is an online digital library that gives you full access to over 5,000 books and videos, as well as industry leading tools to help you plan your personal development and advance your career. For more information, please visit our website.

Why subscribe?

- Spend less time learning and more time coding with practical eBooks and Videos from over 4,000 industry professionals

- Improve your learning with Skill Plans built especially for you

- Get a free eBook or video every month

- Mapt is fully searchable

- Copy and paste, print, and bookmark content

Packt.com

Did you know that Packt offers eBook versions of every book published, with PDF and ePub files available? You can upgrade to the eBook version at `www.packt.com` and as a print book customer, you are entitled to a discount on the eBook copy. Get in touch with us at `customercare@packtpub.com` for more details.

At `www.packt.com`, you can also read a collection of free technical articles, sign up for a range of free newsletters, and receive exclusive discounts and offers on Packt books and eBooks.

Contributors

About the authors

Chandra Sekhar Nayak is an experienced Java developer with extensive knowledge of Android development. He has created a lot of Android applications with a large user base. He is an active member of communities around Java and Android. Being a Kotlin enthusiast, he also created a Kotlin User Group in Bengaluru, India, called BlrKotlin. He runs a YouTube channel called Chanse Code. In his spare time, he loves writing blogs.

Rivu Chakraborty is a Google Certified Android Developer, Caster.io instructor, and Kotlin evangelist. With over 6 years' work experience, he is currently working as a Senior Software Engineer (Android) at BYJU'S The Learning App. Rivu considers himself a Kotlin and Android enthusiast-cum-evangelist. He has been using Kotlin since December 2015. Rivu created the KotlinKolkata User Group, and before moving out to Bangalore, was the lead organiser for both the Kotlin Kolkata User Group and GDG Kolkata.
Along with organizing events, he also speaks at events and conferences in India, including DroidJam India (India's premiere Android conference) and a couple of DevFests. Rivu has authored multiple books on Kotlin and Android development.

About the reviewer

Ranga Rao Karanam is the founder of in 28 Minutes. He is a programmer, trainer, and architect. His areas of interest include cloud-native applications, microservices, evolutionary design, high-quality code, DevOps, BDD, TDD, and refactoring. He loves consulting for start-ups on developing scalable, component-based, cloud-native applications, and following modern development practices such as BDD, continuous delivery, and DevOps.

Ranga started in 28 Minutes with the vision of creating high-quality courses on developing cloud-native Java applications. He is looking forward to enhancing his already considerable success—250,000 students on Udemy and 60,000 subscribers on YouTube. Ranga likes to play cricket and go hiking. His dream is to spend a year hiking the Himalayas.

Packt is searching for authors like you

If you're interested in becoming an author for Packt, please visit `authors.packtpub.com` and apply today. We have worked with thousands of developers and tech professionals, just like you, to help them share their insight with the global tech community. You can make a general application, apply for a specific hot topic that we are recruiting an author for, or submit your own idea.

Table of Contents

Section 4: Modern and Advanced Data Structures

Preface

Data structures and algorithms are more than just theoretical concepts. Learning about them helps you to understand computational complexity, solve problems, and write efficient code. The concepts demonstrate how to design particular algorithm with a real-world implementation.

We will learn about important data structures such as lists, arrays, queues, and stacks, designing some algorithms with real-life implementations, identifying appropriate tools for specific scenarios, and delivering immediate results. Kotlin's data structures and algorithms help you to write code that runs faster.

This book can be used as an end-to-end guide to solve complex problems in your daily development scenarios and will take you through techniques and real-world examples for creating apps in your regular production environment.

Who this book is for

This books is for Kotlin developers who want to dive deep into the Kotlin language and learn the intricacies of implementing data structures and algorithms for scalable application development.

What this book covers

Chapter 1, *A Walk Through – Data Structures and Algorithms*, examines the basic definition of data structures and algorithms, how we can classify them, and their importance.

Chapter 2, *Arrays – First Step to Grouping Data*, dives deep into the most basic data structure, called an array. We will look at different types of arrays, and how to create and use them with some examples.

Chapter 3, *Introducing Linked Lists*, covers different topics on linked lists, their types, and how to implement these different types. It offers a guide on when to use these lists, and how they are different from vectors or lists.

Chapter 4, *Understanding Stacks and Queues*, covers topics related to stacks and queues, how to implement them using arrays, and their use cases. We will start by introducing stacks, then see how to create them using arrays, with some examples showing operations we can make on stacks. Then, we will introduce the queue data structure to the reader, and show them how to implement different types of queues using arrays.

Chapter 5, *Maps – Working with Key-value Pairs*, examines different types of map data structure and when each one is useful. Then, we will implement custom maps to show the reader how they can achieve it.

Chapter 6, *Deep-Dive into Searching Algorithms*, considers algorithms. Since we have already learned a lot of basic data structures, we will be now be introduced to a few algorithms to understand how they can be used to do some operations on those data structures in a more efficient way. We will cover our first and most important operation on different data structures (that is, searching) in this chapter, and also explain different types of searching techniques.

Chapter 7, *Understanding Sorting Algorithms*, explains how to sort a collection of items, and outlines why and when they should be sorted. Then, we will learn different techniques for sorting.

Chapter 8, *Collections and Data Operations in Kotlin*, introduces the collection framework provided by Kotlin and explains its usage to make your work much easier.

Chapter 9, *Introduction to Functional Programming*, introduces the reader to the functional style of writing programs and explains why this is beneficial. We will introduce functional data structures, along with arrow, the functional companion to the Kotlin standard library.

To get the most out of this book

A basic knowledge of the Kotlin language is required to understand the working of the examples.

Download the example code files

You can download the example code files for this book from your account at www.packtpub.com. If you purchased this book elsewhere, you can visit www.packtpub.com/support and register to have the files emailed directly to you.

You can download the code files by following these steps:

1. Log in or register at www.packtpub.com.
2. Select the **SUPPORT** tab.
3. Click on **Code Downloads & Errata**.
4. Enter the name of the book in the **Search** box and follow the onscreen instructions.

Once the file is downloaded, please make sure that you unzip or extract the folder using the latest version of:

- WinRAR/7-Zip for Windows
- Zipeg/iZip/UnRarX for Mac
- 7-Zip/PeaZip for Linux

The code bundle for the book is also hosted on GitHub at https://github.com/ PacktPublishing/Hands-On-Data-Structures-and-Algorithms-with-Kotlin. In case there's an update to the code, it will be updated on the existing GitHub repository.

We also have other code bundles from our rich catalog of books and videos available at https://github.com/PacktPublishing/. Check them out!

Download the color images

We also provide a PDF file that has color images of the screenshots/diagrams used in this book. You can download it here: https://www.packtpub.com/sites/default/files/ downloads/9781788994019_ColorImages.pdf

Conventions used

There are a number of text conventions used throughout this book.

CodeInText: Indicates code words in text, database table names, folder names, filenames, file extensions, pathnames, dummy URLs, user input, and Twitter handles. Here is an example: "When we talk about Kotlin, an array here's represented by a class called Array present in a kotlin package."

A block of code is set as follows:

```
val x = 10
val y = x * 2
for (i in 0..y) {
```

```
    if (i % 2 == 0) {
      println("$i is Even")
    } else {
        println("$i is Odd")
    }
  }
```

When we wish to draw your attention to a particular part of a code block, the relevant lines or items are set in bold:

```
data class User(val firstName: String,
      val lastName: String,
      val phone: String,
      val email: String)
```

Any command-line input or output is written as follows:

```
kotlinc <filename>.kt -include-runtime -d <filename>.jar
```

Bold: Indicates a new term, an important word, or words that you see onscreen. For example, words in menus or dialog boxes appear in the text like this. Here is an example: "Select **System info** from the **Administration** panel."

Warnings or important notes appear like this.

Tips and tricks appear like this.

Get in touch

Feedback from our readers is always welcome.

General feedback: Email feedback@packtpub.com and mention the book title in the subject of your message. If you have questions about any aspect of this book, please email us at questions@packtpub.com.

Errata: Although we have taken every care to ensure the accuracy of our content, mistakes do happen. If you have found a mistake in this book, we would be grateful if you would report this to us. Please visit www.packtpub.com/submit-errata, selecting your book, clicking on the Errata Submission Form link, and entering the details.

Piracy: If you come across any illegal copies of our works in any form on the Internet, we would be grateful if you would provide us with the location address or website name. Please contact us at `copyright@packtpub.com` with a link to the material.

If you are interested in becoming an author: If there is a topic that you have expertise in and you are interested in either writing or contributing to a book, please visit `authors.packtpub.com`.

Reviews

Please leave a review. Once you have read and used this book, why not leave a review on the site that you purchased it from? Potential readers can then see and use your unbiased opinion to make purchase decisions, we at Packt can understand what you think about our products, and our authors can see your feedback on their book. Thank you!

For more information about Packt, please visit `packtpub.com`.

Section 1: Getting Started with Data Structures

This section will walk you through the basics of data structures and will answer your query about why we need to learn data structures and algorithms. You will also learn about the efficiencies of algorithms and how to measure them. Yes, you read that right: Algorithms also have efficiencies, given that they are based on time complexities (execution time needed) and space complexities (memory footprints).

The following chapters will be covered in this section:

- Chapter 1, *A Walk-through – Data Structures and Algorithms*
- Chapter 2, *Arrays – The First Step to Grouping Data*

A Walk Through - Data Structures and Algorithms 1

This book is written with the objective of making you understand what an algorithm is and the importance of it in computer science. Since an algorithm becomes more powerful when used with proper data structures, we'll also walk you through various commonly used data structures in programming.

In this chapter, we're going to focus on theoretical definitions of algorithms and data structures. As we move forward, we'll learn about this in detail.

As this book's title says, we're going to use the Kotlin programming language in all of the examples provided here. You may be asking why Kotlin? Why not any other programming language? The answer would be that it's just a language preference. But as far as algorithms are concerned, they can be understood and practiced with any programming language.

This chapter will help us to understand the following topics:

- Algorithms and their importance
- The efficiency of an algorithm
- Data structures
- Complexity and notations, including Big O notation

Technical requirements

To practice the algorithms and data structures we'll learn from this book, we need the Kotlin compiler to be installed on our PC. There are many ways to set your PC up for this. Let's look into that. Here is the GitHub link of this book:

The GitHub URL for the chapter is here:

```
https://github.com/PacktPublishing/Hands-On-Data-Structures-and-Algorithms-
with-Kotlin/tree/master/Chapter01
```

Working with the command-line compiler

The Kotlin binary is released over GitHub. So you need to find the latest release and download the ZIP file if you want to install the Kotlin compiler manually. Currently, the latest release is 1.2.40, which can be found at this GitHub URL: `https://github.com/JetBrains/kotlin/releases/tag/v1.2.40`. After the Kotlin compiler has downloaded, unzip the downloaded ZIP file into a directory and add the `bin` directory to your system path. This is the directory that contains all of the scripts to compile and run your code.

If you want to install the compiler via SDKMAN, Homebrew, or similar tools, then you can follow the official instruction mentioned here:

```
https://kotlinlang.org/docs/tutorials/command-line.html.
```

To write Kotlin code, you can use any of your favorite editors and start writing. Once the code is written, you can save the file as `<filename>.kt` and it's ready for compilation. Please note that Kotlin files are represented with the `.kt` extension.

For compiling the Kotlin code, you need to use the following command:

```
kotlinc <filename>.kt -include-runtime -d <filename>.jar
```

To run it, use the following command:

```
java -jar <filename>.jar
```

Working with IntelliJ IDEA

If you're comfortable with IDEs and want to use an IDE instead of a simple text editor, then you can choose IntelliJ IDEA as it works seamlessly with Kotlin. The steps for using Kotlin with IntelliJ IDEA are explained in the official documentation here: `https://kotlinlang.org/docs/tutorials/getting-started.html`.

Working with Eclipse

If you're more familiar with Eclipse than IntelliJ IDEA, then follow the official documentation at `https://kotlinlang.org/docs/tutorials/getting-started-eclipse.html` and set it up.

Learning about algorithms

In computer programming, the sole purpose of building any software is to solve a problem existing in the real world and make the world a better place to live in. When we talk about a solution to a problem, it's obvious that we're talking about the procedure to be followed to solve the problem.

Let's consider a case where your teacher comes to you and gives you a bunch of candy, asking you to distribute it equally among your classmates. If you consider this as a problem and try to achieve it with ease, then you might do it as follows:

1. Count the number of candies you have.
2. Count the number of students present in your class.
3. Calculate how many candies should be given to each student.
4. Ask all of the students form a queue so that no student can take the required candies twice.
5. Start distributing the candies to each student.
6. Maintain a separate group for students who already took candies.

As you can see, I've created six steps to solve the task. You might solve it in a different way. These steps are what we call algorithms in computer science.

So, in a nutshell, we can define algorithms as something that takes a value or a set of values as input, processes it, and returns a value or a set of values as output. In other words, we can say that algorithms are a solution to a well-defined computational problem.

In this book, we'll cover the most commonly used basic algorithms, for example, sorting algorithms, searching algorithms, hashing algorithms, and so on.

A few examples of algorithms

Let's look at some examples to understand algorithms. Consider the following code:

```kotlin
private fun add(x: Int, y: Int) = x + y
```

 Please be sure that you have a basic understanding of Kotlin and its syntax.

In the preceding code snippet, the code accepts two arguments as input and returns their sum as output. It satisfies the definition of the algorithm by taking some input, processing the input, and returning the result. Now, consider the following code:

```kotlin
val hourInMillis = 24 * 60 * 60 * 1000
```

In the preceding example, we can still argue that this is an algorithm. Here, the compiler takes 24, 60, 60, and 1000 as input and multiplies all of them to get the single output and finally assigns the output back to the property named `hoursInMillis`. Even though this type of code has nothing to do with the runtime, we can define this as a **compile-time algorithm**.

So, in conclusion, we can say that programs that solve complex computation problems aren't the only programs that can be called **algorithms**. Instead, any program (whether simple or complex), if that consumes some input to calculate and gives some output can be called as an algorithm. For example, sorting and searching aren't the only processes that can be called algorithms; even a simple assignment can also be treated as an algorithm.

This is the beauty of computer science theory. There's no single definition available for algorithms. We just have a few rules to categorize something as an algorithm. As long as your program satisfies those, we can argue that it's an algorithm.

Introduction to data structures

We solved the previous example by taking a few steps, such as asking all students to stand in a queue and, once a student got candy, we moved them to a separate group. We could have also done the same task without asking them to maintain a queue or separating them into a separate group once they got the candy. But we did that to make the task go smoother. Of course, we could have done the task without these two sub-tasks, but that would have created a lot of confusion and made it tedious to finish the task on time.

If we consider that example, we can treat candies and students as data. And to solve the problem given by the teacher, we first structured the data and solved it with ease. This is what we call data structures in computer science.

In this book, we'll cover the most commonly used data structures such as an array, string, list, linked list, stack, queue, tree, graph, and so on. The order isn't the same though. If we talk about data structures in front of others, people generally think about the earlier mentioned data structures. But this doesn't mean that these are the only data structures available. We've a lot more data structures available and ones that are commonly used. In addition to these commonly used data structures, we can also define our own data structures based on our business needs. We might customize data structures in two ways:

- Extend existing data structures
- Customize data structures

If we've a problem, that can be achieved with the help of list but with a slight modification, then we'll try to extend the existing `List` class present in Kotlin's collection framework instead of creating a completely new data structure. For example, the problem statement says to have a list of names, only in uppercase. Of course, there's no existing data structure that can do this out of the box. So you need to extend the `List` and modify it a bit as per our need. So that all existing functionality of `List` gets inherited and works the same as earlier, except with the modified one. Let's see the code:

```
class UpperCasedList : ArrayList<String>() {

    override fun add(element: String): Boolean {
        return super.add(element.toUpperCase())
    }

    override fun add(index: Int, element: String) {
        super.add(index, element.toUpperCase())
    }

    override fun addAll(elements: Collection<String>): Boolean {
        return super.addAll(elements.map { it -> it.toUpperCase() })
```

```
        }

        override fun addAll(index: Int, elements: Collection<String>):
            Boolean {
            return super.addAll(index, elements.map {
                it -> it.toUpperCase() })
        }

        override fun set(index: Int, element: String): String {
            return super.set(index, element.toUpperCase())
        }
    }
```

If you observe the `UpperCasedList` class, you will find that, instead of implementing every functionality of a list, we just tried to modify the functionality related to item-addition functions since our goal is to make sure the list will always contain names in upper case. So, we just extended the existing `ArrayList` data structure and tried to override the required methods to modify it as per our needs.

We can use our custom data structure like this:

```
fun main(args: Array<String>) {
    val names = UpperCasedList()
    names.add("Chandra")
    names.add("Rivu")
    println("Names in upper case : $names") // Output - [CHANDRA, RIVU]
}
```

There might be many different types of problems you would like to solve, that can't be done using existing data structures or by modifying them. In this case, we need to define our own data structures from scratch. Consider the following code:

```
data class User(val firstName: String,
    val lastName: String,
    val phone: String,
    val email: String)
```

As shown in the preceding example, we need a structure that contains all attributes related to users using the software. These type of data structures can't be present in the existing set of data structures. Since these types of data structures are completely based on your business requirements, it's your responsibility to design them on your own. If you're considering those that can manage a collection of items (array, string, list, tree, graph, and more) and are only eligible to be called data structures, then you might want to rethink. In addition to these previously mentioned structures, custom objects we create for our problems (for example, user, customer, seller, and so on) can also be considered data structures.

Complexity analysis

So far, we've gained a good understanding of what an algorithm is and how data structures can be used in an algorithm to make it work better. In our day-to-day life, any task can be completed in many ways. Similarly, in computer science, any computational problem can be solved using many solutions; in other words, they can be solved using many algorithms. Since we've a one-to-many relationship with respect to the problem versus solutions, we might easily get confused while choosing a solution for a particular problem. This is the time for us to understand how to analyze an algorithm and choose the one that suits our problem.

Whenever we're trying to fix a particular computational problem, it's obvious that we'll consider all possible algorithms that can solve it. But we can't use them all together while writing our solution. In this case, we need to analyze all of the possible algorithms and choose the most appropriate one. Usually, we analyze an algorithm based on time complexity and space complexity.

Analyzing with time complexity

The time complexity of an algorithm defines the time taken by it to produce the output for a given input. It quantifies the time taken by the algorithm; in other words, we can define time complexity as the performance of an algorithm. The better the time complexity, the better the performance of the algorithm.

We can simply argue that, instead of choosing a most performant algorithm for our problem, why can't we just increase the hardware capacity so that it can run the instructions much faster? Though the argument looks valid, it isn't. Even if we increase the hardware capacity, it's still a wise decision to choose the most performant algorithm for any problems we have.

Analyzing with space complexity

The space complexity of an algorithm defines the space (memory) consumed by it to produce the output for a given input. In other words, we can say that the algorithm with better space complexity consumes or requires less memory to execute.

Even for space complexity, we can argue that, instead of choosing an algorithm that requires less memory, we can simply increase the memory of our computer to get rid of this issue. But it's always wise to choose an algorithm that consumes less memory.

Time complexity versus space complexity

We might face many issues while choosing an algorithm for any problem. One such issue is time complexity versus space complexity. We might find the following mentioned behavior of an algorithm:

- Faster in execution and consumes less memory
- Faster in execution but consumes more memory
- Slower in execution but consumes less memory
- Slower in execution and consumes more memory

Out of all of the preceding four behaviors, it's clear that algorithms with the first behavior should always be chosen over others, whereas the fourth behavior should always be avoided as much as possible. If we end up with algorithms of the second or third behavior being chosen for solving our problem, then we should choose one of them as per the need. Let's consider that you have a problem, that can be solved using two different algorithms; one algorithm is faster but consumes more memory whereas the other one consumes less memory but is slower in execution. In such a situation, you need to decide which algorithm best suits your requirements. You may need to ask yourself a question, and that is—is solving and replying faster more important, or solving with less memory?

There are lots of tools available in our software world that can measure how much time is taken by an algorithm (a function) and how much memory it consumed. Usually, these tools are called **profilers**. If a profiler can measure the time and space complexity of an algorithm we're writing, then why do we need to study them? The simple answer to this is profilers can measure time complexity in terms of milliseconds or nanoseconds and space complexity in terms of a number of bytes or bits consumed, whereas complexity analysis isn't meant to measure an algorithm the same way a profiler does. Instead, it's used to measure an algorithm at the idea level. For example, the profiler can provide different output about an algorithm when run in two different machines, whereas the complexity analysis of that algorithm tells you the same thing irrespective of the machine you run or the language you code in. By analyzing the complexity of any algorithm, we usually get answers to the following questions:

- How much time does it take to generate or calculate the output?
- How much memory does it need to solve the problem?
- How does it behave when the input size grows?
- Does it get faster or slower? If slower, how much slower? Does it get four times slower for two times the input size?
- What relationship does the time have with respect to the input size?

Learning about notations

So far, we've understood why analyzing the complexity of an algorithm is really important. Now it's time to understand how to analyze the complexity. Before moving ahead with the how-to part, let's understand that, once the complexity of an algorithm is analyzed, there should be some way to represent it. For that, we usually use different notations.

As mentioned earlier, an algorithm can behave differently based on the size of the input given to it. And in the computer world, if you're building software, your algorithm should be prepared for any size of input. So, it's obvious that we need to analyze the complexity of every possible case.

The complexity of an algorithm can broadly fall into the following three categories:

- **Best case analysis**: Best case defines the minimum time required by an algorithm to produce the output. It's also represented as Omega notation (Ω).
- **Average case analysis**: Average case defines the average time required by an algorithm to produce the output for different sized input. It's also represented as Theta notation (θ).
- **Worst case analysis**: Worst case defines the maximum time required by an algorithm to produce the output. It's also represented as a Big O notation (O).

Counting instructions

Before going ahead with examples and explaining the ways we can analyze an algorithm, let's understand how to count the number of instructions present in a particular piece of code.

Let's consider the following example, which identifies the odd and even numbers from 0 to 20 and prints them:

```
val x = 10
val y = x * 2
for (i in 0..y) {
    if (i % 2 == 0) {
        println("$i is Even")
    } else {
        println("$i is Odd")
    }
}
```

Let's break down the code to understand it better, as follows:

- The first line, `val x = 10`, requires one instruction, that is, assigning the value 10 to x.
- The second line, `val y = x * 2`, requires three instructions. The first instruction is to look for x, the second instruction is to multiply it by 2, and the third instruction is to assign the result to y.
- The third line, `for (int i = 0; i < y; i++)`, will run two more instructions in the first iteration of the loop. One is the assignment instruction, `i = 0`, and the other one is the comparison instruction, `i < y`. After the first iteration, there are two more further iterations, that is, `i++` and `i < y`. So the total for instructions here is $4n$.
- From the fourth line onward (the body of the `for` loop), for every iteration, the body will run a few more instructions, such as `i % 2` and result is 0 and then, based on output, print instruction. Moreover, the print instruction is dependent on the result of a condition that itself depends on the condition of the `for` loop. So the total for instructions here is *2n (mod and comp) + 2n (concat and print) = 4n*. Note that the counting of instructions might not be accurate; we're doing it to understand the process. For example, string concat might not be a single instruction. Similarly, printing to console also might have multiple instructions. But we're considering those as one instruction to understand them better.

Asymptotic behavior

We can easily notice that the instructions count is getting tougher and tougher and we don't really need to deal with this tedious process. For example, instead of saying the complexity of the preceding algorithm is *f(n) = 1 + 3 + 4n + 4n = 4 + 8n*, we can simplify it further.

Since our main intention behind analyzing the complexity of an algorithm is to identify how it behaves when the input grows or shrinks, we can ignore the instructions, which are always constant.

In the previous example, *f(n) = 4 + 8n*, it's clear that *4* and *8* never change, so by ignoring those, we can conclude *f(n) = n*. Here, we ignored all of the factors that don't change based on the input and considered only those factors that change based on the input. This is what we call **asymptotic behavior**.

Let's see some examples:

- $f(n) = 3n + 5$ can be considered $f(n) = n$
- $f(n) = 5$ can be considered $f(n) = 1$
- $f(n) = n^2 + 3n + 5$ can be considered $f(n) = n^2$

In simple terms, we can summarize the asymptotic behavior of an algorithm as follows:

- Any program that doesn't have any loop has $f(n) = 1$.
- Any program with one `for` loop has $f(n) = n$.
- Any program with one nested `for` loop (`for` loop inside another `for` loop) has $f(n) = n^2$.

Examples of complexity analysis

With the preceding theory, let's try to analyze the worst, best, and average case of an algorithm. Let's consider an example of searching for an element from a given array. So the code will look as follows:

```
private fun find(input: IntArray, item: Int) {
    for (i in input.indices) {
        if (input[i] == item) {
            print("Item found at index - $i")
        }
    }
}
```

Please note that the preceding code isn't written using proper Kotlin idiomatic syntax purposefully, to make you understand things better.

Let's say the input array is `[1,5,67,56,38,97,34,50,81]` and we're trying to search for the following numbers:

- `1`: This can be found in the first iteration itself. This is an example of the best case.
- `38`: Since it's somewhere in the middle of the input, we can get the result in approximately $n/2$ iterations (n is the length of the input array). This is an example of an average case.
- `81`: Since it;s the last item of the input array, the result will come at the nth iteration.
- `102`: Since it isn't present, the result will be produced at the nth iteration.

As we can see, based on the item we're searching for, the number of iterations are varied. So we should consider all cases during our analysis. Since it's always a best practice to be prepared for the worst, we prefer analyzing the worst case more often. Let's see the final analysis for the preceding search algorithm:

```
Best Case - Ω(1)
Average case - θ(n/2)
Worst case - O(n)
```

Since we don't consider the constant factors while performing complexity analysis, we can consider θ(n/2) as θ(n). But please note that here, O(n) > θ(n).

Summary

So far, we've understood what an algorithm is and how it can be used with any data structures to solve problems easily. We also understood how to analyze the complexity of an algorithm. But this is just the beginning. As the chapters go on, all of the examples we discuss will relate to complexity analysis and similar information.

We will discuss about many commonly used data structures in further chapters and will try to do the complexity analysis for all those data structures and algorithms.

Further reading

- https://kotlinlang.org/docs/tutorials/command-line.html
- https://kotlinlang.org/docs/tutorials/getting-started.html
- https://kotlinlang.org/docs/tutorials/getting-started-eclipse.html

Arrays - First Step to Grouping Data

2

Arrays are one of the most fundamental **Data Structures** (**DS**) commonly used by almost all programmers. An *array* is nothing but a data structure that can store more than one value of the same data type.

By the end of this chapter, we'll understand more about arrays and the following topics:

- Operations with arrays (in Kotlin)
- Dynamic arrays and their operations
- Immutable arrays
- Multidimensional arrays and their operations
- Strings and their related operations

Technical requirements

There are no specific requirements here. To practice the algorithms and data structures we'll learn from this book, we need the Kotlin compiler to be installed on our PC.

The GitHub URL for the chapter is here:

```
https://github.com/PacktPublishing/Hands-On-Data-Structures-and-Algorithms-
with-Kotlin/tree/master/Chapter02.
```

Introduction to arrays

Being a basic data structure, every language supports creating an array. When we talk about Kotlin, an array here's represented by a class called `Array` present in a `kotlin` package. Like other classes, it has a few member functions and properties. Let's see what it looks like using the following code:

```
class Array<T> private constructor() {
    val size: Int
    operator fun get(index: Int): T
    operator fun set(index: Int, value: T): Unit

    operator fun iterator(): Iterator <T>
        // ...
}
```

In terms of the preceding code snippet of the `Array` class defined in the Kotlin core API, we can say that it has a `size` property to tell us the current size of the array; the `get` and `set` functions, which basically overload the `[]` operator; and an `iterator` function to let us iterate over the items.

So, using the preceding mentioned properties, we can see what operations can be done with an array.

Operations with arrays

We can have the following possible operations for an array:

- Creating an array
- Fetching elements from an array
- Iterating an array
- Updating elements in an array

In the following sections of this chapter, we'll understand all of these operations with examples.

Creating an array

In Kotlin, an array can be created in the following two ways:

- Using library functions
- Using the constructor of the `Array<T>` class

Creating an array using library functions

Kotlin provides many library functions, which help us into create arrays in a seamless manner. For example, to create an array of strings, we can use the `arrayOf` function and pass the string values over it. Consider the following example.

Let's store all of my friends' names into a single data structure, and then we can store them in an array of strings. Let's look at some code to understand how we can create an array:

```
val friends = arrayOf("Rivu", "Subin", "Sid", "Susri", "Ramya",
"Sachin")
```

The preceding snippet is the way we create an array of strings in Kotlin. As I have more than one friend and all of their names are strings, this satisfies all of the characteristics of an array. Let's look at the following example:

```
val info = arrayOf("Rivu", 32, 5.11, "rivu@abc.com")
```

The preceding snippet is a way to create an array of any in Kotlin. Though it isn't recommended to create an array of `Any` for the mentioned purpose, it's shown to make you understand that it's possible. Here, all of the items of an array are of a different type, but still, we're able to create an array because all of them are a subclass of `Any`. Now, let's try to modify the preceding example a bit and let's see what happens:

```
val info: Array<String> = arrayOf("Rivu", 32, 5.11, "rivu@abc.com")
```

This example is the same as the preceding one with an added type. Since the type of the array is mentioned as `String`, it's mandatory to have all of the elements of the array be `String` or any subclass of `String`. Since the first and second indexes are neither `String` nor any subtype of `String`, the preceding code will fail to compile.

From the previous three examples, we can conclude that arrays in Kotlin can be created only if all of the items are of the same type (first example) or a subtype of a single type (second example).

There could be many scenarios where we need different types of arrays to be created. Just discussing the previous three examples might not enough. So let's try to find all of those types of arrays via a quiz, where you ask all of your questions and I will try to answer:

- How do I create an array of numbers? The same way as mentioned earlier:

```
val numbers = arrayOf(1, 3, 5, 7, 9)
```

- An array in Kotlin is represented by a class called `Array`. Then how does a class with the generic type, `<T>`, represent primitive type array?
- The preceding example will create an array of `Integer`, the wrapper type and not the primitive type.
- Then how do I create an array of primitive numbers? For creating a primitive numbered array, we've special library functions:

```
val oddNums = intArrayOf(1, 3, 5, 7, 9)
```

- Is this function's return type the same as the preceding one? No. Since the `Array` class has a generic parameter, it can't represent a primitive typed array. For those, we've classes such as `IntArray, ByteArray, LongArray`, and so on. And the corresponding arrays can be created using library functions: `intArrayOf, byteArrayOf, longArrayOf`, and so on.
- How do I create an array of a custom object? The same way we created an array of strings:

```
val users = arrayOf(
    User("Chandra Sekhar", "Nayak", "0909090909",
"chansek@live.com"),
    User("Utkarsh", "Asthana", "1234123412", "utku@xyz.com"),
    User("Sachin", "Kamble", "7878787878", "sachin@abc.com"),
    User("Ramya", "K", "0000000000", "ramu@zzz.com"),
    User("Subin", "S", "1234512345", "sub@s.com")
)
```

 The `User` class was created in the `Chapter 1`, *A Walk Through Data Structures and Algorithms*. You should import the respective `User` class to make the preceding snippet compile.

- All of the examples discussed are when you know the values an array should be initialized with. What if I don't know the values up-front during array initialization? In this case, you can create an array by assigning null values, then set the value after it gets ready.

- Can you show me an example of initializing an array with null values? We can do this using the same `arrayOf` function:

```
val serverUsers: Array<User?> = arrayOf(null, null, null, null,
null)
```

The type of the array is `User` as we can't assign `null` to a non-nullable type in Kotlin (for example, `User`).

If we initialize an array with null values this way, though it works fine, it's tedious to do so. As the required size of the array is more, that any number of times you need to repeat null arguments in the `arrayOf` function. Imagine using `arrayOf (null, null, ... 100 times null)`. To avoid this situation, we've a very convenient utility function. Let's have a look at that:

```
val biggerNullArray: Array<User?> = arrayOfNulls(100)
```

The preceding snippet just creates an array of a size of `100` and initializes all items with `null` without us doing the tedious job.

Creating an array using the constructor

We've already discussed previously that, in Kotlin, arrays are represented by the `Array<T>` class but, as the previous examples showed, to create an array is so far by using the `arrayOf` and similar library functions. Since `Array<T>` is a class, there should be some way to create its object using the constructor. Let's see how to do it in the following example:

```
val squares = Array(51, {i -> i * i})
```

The preceding snippet creates an array of squares of numbers up to 50. You may notice that the constructor of the `Array` class takes a function along with the size as arguments, so we can literally pass any function that evaluates the initial value of the element we want. For more examples, please refer the GitHub repository associated with this chapter: https://github.com/PacktPublishing/Hands-On-Data-Structures-and-Algorithms-with-Kotlin/tree/master/Chapter02 .

The second argument of the preceding snippet is a Lambda expression. It's a short replacement for the anonymous inner class. You can find more examples of it in Chapter 8, *Collections and Data Operations in Kotlin*, and Chapter 7, *Understanding Sorting Algorithms*.

Accessing elements from an array

Accessing any element from an array in Kotlin can be done in the following three ways:

- Using the Array Access Operator, `[]`
- Using the `get` function
- Using extension functions

Accessing an element using the Array Access Operator `[]`

Like other languages, accessing any element from an array is done using the Array Access Operator, `[]`. To understand this more, refer to the following examples.

We need to revisit one of the previous examples to demonstrate this. Let's pick the array that stores a few programming language names and accesses a few elements from it, as follows:

```
val languages = arrayOf("Kotlin", "Java", "C", "C++", "C#",
"JavaScript")
val firstLanguage = languages[0]
val fifthLanguage = languages[4]
```

The previous examples will work provided that the index passed into the Array Access Operator, `[]`, is valid. Check this using the following code:

```
val invalidLanguage = languages[-1]
val outLanguage = languages[100]
```

Though the preceding snippet looks fine syntactically, it isn't correct. While accessing any element from an array, we should be aware of its index inside the array. A valid index of an array is from 0 to $n-1$, where *n* is the size of the given array. Since the preceding snippet has both lines with an invalid index, in both these cases we'll get a `java.lang.ArrayIndexOutOfBoundsException` runtime exception.

Accessing an element using the get function

Since an array in Kotlin is represented by the `Array` class, we can ask a question: how does a class support an operator, `[]`, to let the user access its properties? It's possible in Kotlin because of Kotlin's support for *operator overloading*. So, whenever we try to use `val item = array[0]`, it internally calls the `get` function defined in the `Array` class and returns the desired result. Since the Kotlin compiler accesses an element by internally calling the `get` function, we should also be able to call it directly. The following example shows you how:

```
val secondLanguage = languages.get(1)
val sixthLanguage = languages.get(5)
```

You can compare both these methods to understand that the behavior is absolutely the same; just the syntax is different.

Accessing an element using the extension functions

The `Array` class has a few extension functions, which helps us to access an element from an array with ease. A few of them are `component1()`, `component2()`, `component3()`, `component4()`, and `component5()`. These functions return the 1st, 2nd, 3rd, 4th, and 5th element of the array respectively. Consider the following example:

```
val firstLang = languages.component1()
val secLang = languages.component2()
```

Like component functions, it also has a few more functions such as `elementAt()`, `elementAtOrElse()`, `elementAtOrNull()`, `getOrElse()`, and `getOrNull()`, which do the same job. Consider the following code:

```
val firstItem = languages.elementAt(0)
val secItem = languages.elementAt(0)
val tenthItem = languages.elementAtOrElse(9, {_ -> "Not Available"})
val eleventhItem = languages.elementAtOrNull(10)
```

These are just utility functions to help us to write more readable code, but internally these functions use corresponding `get` functions to do the job for us.

Iterating over an array

So far, we've looked at creating an array and accessing elements from the array. But accessing elements one by one doesn't help much. Most of the time, we need access to every element of an array to do our job. Imagine an array of a size of one million; we cannot write one million lines of code to access those elements and maintain those one million variables. This is where iterating over an array comes in handy.

Iterating over an array can be done in three ways:

- Using loops (`for`, `while`, and so on)
- Using an iterator
- Using extension functions

Let's see some examples explaining the usage of the preceding options:

```
for (i in languages.indices) {
    if (i % 2 == 0) {
        println(languages[i])
    } else {
        println(languages[i].toUpperCase())
    }
}
```

The preceding method will allow you to access an array with the help of its indices. There might be many situations where you need to decide based on the index of the element. For these situations, this works well.

If you want to avoid getting the index and accessing the value through the index separately, then you can use an extension function to destroy both of these. Let's look at the following example:

```
for ((index, value) in languages.withIndex()) {
    if (index % 2 == 0) {
        println("The element at $index is $value")
    } else {
        println("The element at $index is ${value.toUpperCase()}")
    }
}
```

If you don't have any need for the index, then you can iterate with a much easier method, as follows:

```
for (language in languages) {
    println("Language - $language")
}
```

In addition to all of the preceding mentioned standard way of iterating an array, Kotlin also has lots of extension functions that let us write idiomatic functional style of programming. Consider the following code:

```
languages.forEach {
    println("Language in Upper Case - ${it.toUpperCase()}")
}
```

`forEach` is not the only extension function in Kotlin to manage the array in an idiomatic, functional style. To find all of the list of functions available, refer to this URL: `https://kotlinlang.org/api/latest/jvm/stdlib/kotlin/-array/index.html`.

Updating elements in an array

Similar to how we can access any element of an array in several ways, updating any element can also be done in the following ways:

- Using the Array Access Operator, `[]`
- Using the `set` function
- Using extension functions

Look at the following example, which demonstrates all of these options:

```
languages[1] = "Swift"
languages[4] = "Objective-C"
println("Newly updated languages are - ${Arrays.toString(languages)}")

// output - Newly updated languages are - [Kotlin, Swift, C, C++,
Objective-C, JavaScript, Python]
```

In the preceding snippet, we've tried to update the first and fourth indexed values with a new value using the Array Access Operator, `[]`.

We can also achieve the same using the `set` function as follows:

```
languages.set(5, "TypeScript")
languages.set(6, "Dart")
println("Newly updated languages are - ${Arrays.toString(languages)}")

// Output - Newly updated languages are - [Kotlin, Swift, C, C++,
Objective-C, TypeScript, Dart]
```

Vectors (dynamic arrays)

One of the most common problems we face while working with arrays is that we need to know the size of the array during its initialization. It isn't possible to know the size of the array up-front during its initialization. Imagine a case where you're building a social networking project, and you're trying to fetch all of the friends of a particular user from the server and display these in the UI. The number of friends that a user has can't be known unless we get the response from the server. These kinds of situations can be handled using vectors.

A *vector* is nothing but a data structure backed by an array, which can grow in size when required. Let's try to build a simple implementation of the Vector class to understand it more:

```kotlin
class Vector <E> {
    private val minCapacityIncrement = 12
    var elements: Array <Any?>
    private var size = 0

    constructor() {
        this.elements = arrayOf()
    }

    constructor(initialCapacity: Int) {
        if (initialCapacity > 0) {
            this.elements = Array(initialCapacity) {
                i -> null
            }
        } else if (initialCapacity == 0) {
            this.elements = emptyArray()
        } else {
            throw IllegalArgumentException("Illegal Capacity:
$initialCapacity")
        }
    }

    fun add(element: E): Boolean {
        // check below for implementation detail
    }

    fun add(index: Int, element: E) {
        // check below for implementation detail
    }

    fun get(index: Int): E {
        // check below for implementation detail
```

```
    }

    fun set(index: Int, element: E): E {
        // check below for implementation detail
    }

    fun remove(index: Int): E {
        // check below for implementation detail
    }

    fun remove(element: E): Boolean {
        // check below for implementation detail
    }

    // This method is called by other public APIs explained below
    private fun newCapacity(currentCapacity: Int): Int {
        val increment =
            if (currentCapacity < minCapacityIncrement / 2)
                minCapacityIncrement
            else
                currentCapacity shr 1
        return currentCapacity + increment
    }

    private fun throwIndexOutOfBoundsException(index: Int, size: Int):
    IndexOutOfBoundsException {
        throw IndexOutOfBoundsException("Invalid index $index, size is
$size")
    }
}
```

Adding an element to a Vector class

Adding an element can be exposed to two different APIs—a simple API that takes an element as input and inserts it into the last index, add(element: E), and another API that takes an index as an additional input, add(index: Int, element: E). Let's look into the first one:

```
fun add(element: E): Boolean {
    var a = elements
    val s = size
    if (s == a.size) {
        val newArray = arrayOfNulls<Any> (s +
            if (s < minCapacityIncrement / 2)
                minCapacityIncrement
            else
```

```
                    s shr 1)
        System.arraycopy(a, 0, newArray, 0, s)
        a = newArray
        elements = a
    }
    a[s] = element
    size = s + 1
    return true
}
```

If you observe the preceding implementation, you can see that the function is capable of adding the given element to the backup array even though the initial or current size of the array doesn't fit. It does this by creating a larger array and copying the existing elements. Check the code inside the `if (s == a.size)` size-checking condition.

The other API with an index also does a similar job with a small difference in array copy implementation. Here's the code:

```
fun add(index: Int, element: E) {
    var a = elements
    val s = size
    if (index > s || index < 0) {
        throwIndexOutOfBoundsException(index, s)
    }
    if (s < a.size) {
        System.arraycopy(a, index, a, index + 1, s - index)
    } else {
        val newArray = arrayOfNulls<Any>(newCapacity(s))
        System.arraycopy(a, 0, newArray, 0, index)
        System.arraycopy(a, index, newArray, index + 1, s - index)
        a = newArray
        elements = a
    }
    a[index] = element
    size = s + 1
}
```

The preceding snippet executes as follows:

1. It checks the size and throws an exception if not valid.
2. If the backed-up array has the capacity, it moves every element from the given index to its next index.

3. If the backed-up array is full, it creates a larger array and copies the existing elements into a new array in two phases:
    1. Copies elements from 0th index to the given index
    2. Copies elements from the next index to the last index
4. Finally, it puts the given element into the given index.

Updating and fetching an element

These two APIs have the simplest implementation. A vector stores its elements in an array; we just validate the given index and either update or return the element if valid. Here's the code:

```
fun get(index: Int): E {
    if (index >= size) throwIndexOutOfBoundsException(index, size)
    return elements[index] as E
}

fun set(index: Int, element: E): E {
    if (index >= size) throwIndexOutOfBoundsException(index, size)
    val oldValue = elements[index] as E
    elements[index] = element
    return oldValue
}
```

Removing an element from Vector

APIs such as add are not the only functions that resize the array; there are many more functions in the Vector implementation that resize the backup array. The remove API also resizes the array by making it smaller. The remove API can also be exposed in two different ways. One API takes the element as input, which should be removed, remove(element: E), and the other takes the index whose element should be removed, remove(index: Int). Let's look into the code:

```
fun remove(index: Int): E {
    if (index >= size) throwIndexOutOfBoundsException(index, size)
    val oldValue = elements[index] as E
    val numMoved = size - index - 1
    if (numMoved > 0)
        System.arraycopy(elements, index + 1, elements, index, numMoved)
    elements[--size] = null // clear to let GC do its work
    return oldValue
}
```

The preceding code clearly shows how we rearrange the array elements while removing the element. If you closely observe the implementation, you will see that it looks similar to the add API.

The other API code does the same thing as shown earlier, with an additional search for the given element. Here's the code:

```
fun remove(element: E): Boolean {
    for (index in 0 until size) {
        if (element == elements[index]) {
            val numMoved = size - index - 1
            if (numMoved > 0)
                System.arraycopy(elements, index + 1, elements, index,
numMoved)
            elements[--size] = null // clear to let GC do its work
            return true
        }
    }
    return false
}
```

We've seen a simpler implementation of the dynamic array, but this is not the only way you can implement it. You can achieve this in many ways based on your needs. Moreover, you can add many more functions in addition to the add, remove, and set functions.

 The previously mentioned Vector implementation is not fully completed. It has a few major capabilities such as adding an element, setting an element at a given index, and removing an element. For the full implementation, check out our GitHub repository at https://github.com/PacktPublishing/Hands-On-Data-Structures-and-Algorithms-with-Kotlin.

As working with dynamic arrays is a very common use case in software, all programming languages, including Kotlin, have already done it for us. As long as you don't have any specific use case that can't be solved by the default implementation, you might not have to reinvent the wheel and create the same for your project. Let's see some examples using the default implementation:

```
val companies = arrayListOf<String>("Google", "Microsoft", "Facebook",
"Apple", "JetBrains")

companies.add("Amazon")
companies.add("Samsung")

companies.set(2, "Twitter")
```

```
companies.remove("Samsung")
companies.removeAt(2)
```

From the preceding snippet, you can easily understand that this does the exact same thing that our previous example is able to do. Moreover, this is more hassle free as we don't need to create any class for it.

 Like the `arrayOf()` function we discussed earlier, to create a dynamic array, we use the `arrayListOf()` function. In Kotlin, instead of calling it as a dynamic array or `Vector`, we call it as `ArrayList`.

The beauty of immutable arrays

Immutability is one of the key principles of modern programming languages. So, it's obvious that Kotlin also has immutability implementation. Because of this, Kotlin's collections package has treated immutable data structures as first-class citizens. A few examples might make you understand this more:

```
val days = listOf("Sunday", "Monday", "Tuesday", "Wednesday")
val months = arrayListOf("January", "February", "March", "April")
```

In the preceding snippet, `days` is an immutable list whereas `months` is a mutable one. For example, `months.add("May")` is a valid statement whereas we cannot add an item to the `days` list. The only way to do so is to get a new list out of the existing one by adding the new item. Here's the method:

```
val modifiedDays = days + "Thursday"
months.add("May")
```

The first statement in the preceding snippet creates a new list and that too is an immutable one. So if we try to print both `days` and `modifiedDays`, then the output will be as follows:

```
Days - [Sunday, Monday, Tuesday, Wednesday]
Modified Days - [Sunday, Monday, Tuesday, Wednesday, Thursday]
```

Like `list`, Kotlin also separates mutable data structures and immutable data structures completely. Here's a table describing those:

Kotlin functions	Description
`listOf()`	Creates an immutable list
`arrayListOf()`	Creates a mutable list
`mutableListOf()`	Creates a mutable list
`setOf()`	Creates an immutable set
`mutableSetOf()`	Creates a mutable set
`mapOf()`	Creates an immutable map
`mutableMapOf()`	Creates a mutable map

To be a good programmer, we should always use immutable data structures and try to use them as much as possible if our use case holds good. Kotlin already provides many ways to use immutable data structures out of the box. But for our understanding, let's try to create an immutable list and explore the world of immutability with the following code:

```kotlin
class ImmutableList<E> {
    private val minCapacityIncrement = 12
    var elements: Array <Any?>
    private var size = 0

    constructor() {
        this.elements = arrayOf()
    }

    constructor(initialCapacity: Int) {
        if (initialCapacity > 0) {
            this.elements = Array(initialCapacity) { _ -> null}
        } else if (initialCapacity == 0) {
            this.elements = emptyArray()
        } else {
            throw IllegalArgumentException("Illegal Capacity:
$initialCapacity")
        }
    }

    constructor(vararg items: E) {
        this.elements = items as Array <Any?>
        size = items.size
    }
```

Here we're returning a new object instead of mutating the same:

```
fun add(element: E): ImmutableList<E> {
    val s = size
    val newList = ImmutableList<E> (s + 1)
    System.arraycopy(elements, 0, newList.elements, 0, s)
    newList.elements[s] = element
    newList.size = s + 1
    return newList
}

fun get(index: Int): E {
    if (index >= size)
        throwIndexOutOfBoundsException(index, size)
    return elements[index] as E
}
```

In usual List, we could have updated the element directly. But in this case, we're creating a new object, copying the existing elements into the newly created object and then we update the required element before returning the new object.

```
fun set(index: Int, element: E): ImmutableList<E> {
    if (index >= size)
        throwIndexOutOfBoundsException(index, size)

    val s = size
    val newList = ImmutableList<E> (s)
    System.arraycopy(elements, 0, newList.elements, 0, s)
    newList.elements[index] = element
    newList.size = s
    return newList
}

fun isEmpty() = size == 0

fun size() = size

operator fun contains(element: E): Boolean {
    return indexOf(element) >= 0
}

fun indexOf(element: E): Int {
    if (element == null) {
        for (i in 0 until size)
            if (elements[i] == null)
                return i
    } else {
        for (i in 0 until size)
```

```
                if (element == elements[i])
                    return i
        }
        return -1
    }

    fun lastIndexOf(element: E): Int {
        if (element == null) {
            for (i in size - 1 downTo 0)
                if (elements[i] == null)
                    return i
        } else {
            for (i in size - 1 downTo 0)
                if (element == elements[i])
                    return i
        }
        return -1
    }

    fun toArray(): Array <out Any?> {
        return Arrays.copyOf(elements, size)
    }
```

After that, we check how the capacity works:

```
    private fun newCapacity(currentCapacity: Int): Int {
        val increment = if (currentCapacity < minCapacityIncrement / 2)
                            minCapacityIncrement
                        else
                            currentCapacity shr 1
        return currentCapacity + increment
    }

    private fun throwIndexOutOfBoundsException(index: Int, size: Int):
IndexOutOfBoundsException {
        throw IndexOutOfBoundsException("Invalid index $index, size is
$size")
    }

    override fun toString() = Arrays.toString(elements)
}
```

If you compare it with the previously created `Vector` class, you will find a lot of similarities. A few major differences are as follows:

- The `Vector` class is mutable whereas the `ImmutableList` class is immutable.
- `Vector` had `add`, `set`, and `remove` methods, which were mutating the backed-up array.
- `ImmutableList` has `add` and `set` methods but they create a new `ImmutableList` object and return it to the caller instead of mutating the current object.

 Compare the `add` and `set` methods of both the `Vector` and `ImmutableList` class to understand the way immutable data structures can be implemented.

A few benefits of the immutable data structure are as follows:

- They are thread safe by default.
- They encapsulate their properties better.
- We won't end up with any invalid states while using immutable objects.
- These are easier to test.
- There are better code maintainability and readability.

 CAUTION: Despite saying immutable data structures are good, we cannot just assume that we should always use immutable ones. Both immutable and mutable data structures have their own uses and pros and cons. Depending on our use case, we can choose `any` of the data structures.

Multidimensional array

In Kotlin, a multidimensional array is nothing but an array of arrays. The following example of creating a multidimensional array will give you a better understanding of it:

```
val numbers = arrayOf(
    arrayOf(1, 2, 3),
    arrayOf(4, 5, 6),
    arrayOf(7, 8, 9)
)
```

In the preceding example, the parent array has three elements and all of these items are arrays by themselves. All of the child arrays have three elements each, but it isn't mandatory to have the same number of elements in each child array. Have a look at the following example:

```
val food = arrayOf(
    arrayOf("Apple", "Apricot", "Avocado"),
    arrayOf("Banana", "Broccoli", "Beetroot"),
    arrayOf("Cherry", "Carrot")
)
```

Here, we tried to fill in a few vegetable and fruit names in an array alphabetically. Note that the array at the second index has only two elements in it.

Operations in multidimensional arrays

We can do all of those operations we did with single dimensional arrays. Let's look at those operations in detail.

Accessing an element

Using the Array Access Operator, [], we can access any element, as in the following example:

```
val row1 = food[0]
val row2 = food[1]
```

Both row1 and row2 are 1D arrays representing foods starting with A and B respectively.

If we want to access the elements further, then we can do so, as follows:

```
val firstFoodWithA = row1[0]
val firstFoodWithB = row2[0]
```

We can also access the elements directly without having to get the child arrays and then their elements. Here's an example:

```
println("2nd food item which starts from B is : ${food[1][1]}")
println("2nd food item which starts from C is : ${food[2][1]}")
```

Updating an element

In the same way, we accessed both immediate elements as well as deeper elements, we can update them too. Refer to the following example:

```
food[0] = arrayOf("Date", "Damson", "Durian")
```

The preceding snippet updates the first array with the newly assigned array. We can also update a deeper element, as shown in the following example:

```
food[2][1] = "Coconut"
```

Here, we're updating the element from `Carrot` to `Coconut`.

Iterating over the array

As mentioned earlier when discussing iterating a 1D, this also works the same way. Refer to the following example:

```
for (row in food) {
    print("Item : ")
    for (item in row) {
        print("$item ")
    }
    println()
}
```

Other ways of iterating also go the same way.

Working with a matrix

A matrix has an important role in solving lots of mathematical problems. So, it's obvious that it has much more significance in computer science. We can represent a matrix with an array of arrays in Kotlin. We can program some matrix operations to learn how to use a matrix. As Kotlin allows subarrays of any size, we need to check whether it's a valid matrix or not before going ahead with `any` operation. The following example shows you how to check whether a matrix is valid or not:

```
fun isValidMatrix(arr: Array<Array<*>> ): Boolean {
    var isValid = true
    var sizeOfRow = arr[0].size
    // Can be optimized more by iterating from 1st index instead of 0th
    for (row in arr) {
        if (sizeOfRow != row.size) {
```

```
                isValid = false
                break
        }
    }
    return isValid
}
```

Since we've now validated a matrix, let's try to solve a few basic problems regarding the matrix.

Adding two matrices

In this example, we're going to create a function that takes two matrices as input and returns a matrix by adding both of them:

```
fun add(a: Array<DoubleArray>, b: Array<DoubleArray>):
Array<DoubleArray> {
    val m = a.size
    val n = a[0].size
    val c = Array(m) { DoubleArray(n) }
    for (i in 0 until m)
        for (j in 0 until n)
            c[i][j] = a[i][j] + b[i][j]
    return c
}
```

In this way, you can also do subtraction between two matrices.

Multiplying two matrices

Multiplying two matrices can be different based on the operand. If both matrices are 2D, then the output is a 2D matrix. If either one of those matrices is 1D, then the output is a 1D matrix. Here, we'll see one example:

```
fun multiply(a: Array<DoubleArray>, b: Array<DoubleArray>):
Array<DoubleArray> {
    val m1 = a.size
    val n1 = a[0].size
    val m2 = b.size
    val n2 = b[0].size
    if (n1 != m2) throw RuntimeException("Illegal matrix dimensions.")
    val c = Array(m1) { DoubleArray(n2) }
    for (i in 0 until m1)
        for (j in 0 until n2)
            for (k in 0 until n1)
```

```
                     c[i][j] += a[i][k] * b[k][j]
        return c
    }
```

The preceding mentioned examples are just to give you a brief understanding of how we can perform matrix operations using arrays (1D or 2D). We can still do more with the matrix, which can be practiced by you from the questions mentioned in the exercise.

A short introduction to strings

Like dynamic arrays (`ArrayList`), strings are also represented by a class and have a backup array of characters. Similar to other data structures, strings also can be implemented as mutable and immutable.

Immutable strings in Kotlin are represented by the `String` class, whereas mutable strings are represented by the `StringBuilder` class.

The string class doesn't provide any public API to mutate the backed-up character array. So you can only find APIs such as `elementAt()`, `indexOf()`, and `lastIndexOf()` or similar `get` functions. Though it has mutating APIs such as `subSequence()`, `capitalize()`, or similar, they always create a copy of the string and return the updated one without mutating the existing string.

In the other case, `StringBuilder` offers many mutating APIs such as `append()`, `insert()`, `replace()`, `reverse()`, and many more. These APIs literally update the backed-up array instead of creating a new `StringBuilder` object.

 Note that the `()` in the API names doesn't mean that they're all APIs that don't take `any` arguments. This is mentioned to help you understand that they're methods.

Summary

Linear data structures such as static or dynamic arrays are among those few data structures that are most preferred by many programmers. Though an array is linear and static in nature, by tweaking it for ourselves, we can create different types of data structures around arrays. In this chapter, we tweaked the same static array to create a dynamic array (`Vector`) and an immutable dynamic array (`ImmutableList`).

Since immutability is playing an important role in modern programming languages such as Kotlin, we cannot just blindly go ahead and use immutable data structures everywhere, as long as we aren't understand the difference between mutability and immutability.

We can implement `any` immutable data structure in two ways; the easiest way to implement an immutable data structure is to encapsulate the properties inside the class without using `any` public APIs to modify them for example, no `add`, `set`, or `remove` APIs.

The other way to do so is to create a new object whenever a public mutating API is getting called. Check the add and set methods of the `ImmutableList` class for better understanding.

Matrices also play a vital role in solving many mathematical problems, so we tried to solve a few, and a few more are to be solved by you as your task.

Linear data structures (arrays) aren't only used for managing list of items and manipulating them. In future chapters, we'll understand how they can be used in many more ways.

Questions

1. Create an array of numbers between 0 to 500 that are multiples of 10.
2. Create an array with all the even indexed numbers of given array.
3. Write a snippet for finding a transpose of a matrix.
4. Write a snippet to append elements of two arrays.
5. Write snippet to convert wrapper typed array to a primitive array.

Section 2: Efficient Grouping of Data with Various Data Structures

In this section of the book, you will discuss various popular data structures, including Linked Lists, Stacks, Queues, and Maps. You will learn about the theories behind them, and also about how to implement them using the simplest data structure – an array. You will also learn how to perform simple searching and sorting with these data structures.

The following chapters will be covered in this section:

- Chapter 3, *Introducing Linked Lists*
- Chapter 4, *Understanding Stacks and Queues*
- Chapter 5, *Maps – Working with Key-Value Pairs*

Introducing Linked Lists

3

So far, we've looked at using an array when several items need to be grouped together. But arrays weren't enough to fulfill all of our engineering problems. In most cases, we weren't aware of the number of items we want to group together. So, similar to the saying, *necessity is the mother of invention*, we created a data structure by wrapping an array into a custom class and making it grow able when required. This helped us in grouping multiple items without even knowing their size. We called them **Vector** or **ArrayList**. Though our size requirements are solved by ArrayList, we've a basic problem in ArrayList and that is its performance while inserting. If the ArrayList is full and we try to insert an item, we need to create a bigger array and copy all existing items to the new one, which might take more time if the size is big. This is a problem where `LinkedList` comes into play and solves the insertion problem.

This chapter will look at the following topics:

- Getting started with `LinkedList`
- Understanding a Singly Linked List
- Understanding a Doubly Linked List
- Understanding a Circular Linked List

Technical requirements

There are no specific requirements here. To practice the algorithms and data structures we'll learn from this book, we need the Kotlin compiler to be installed on our PC.

The GitHub URL for the chapter is here:

https://github.com/PacktPublishing/Hands-On-Data-Structures-and-Algorithms-with-Kotlin/tree/master/Chapter03

Getting started with LinkedList

We can define a `LinkedList` as a data structure that's linear in nature and all of the elements establish a link to their next element. These are few properties we can find in a `LinkedList`:

- Along with a value, each element in a `LinkedList` is responsible for holding the reference of the next element.
- As all elements hold multiple things in them, generally they're all objects and are called node instead of the element.
- The first node is called the `head` of the `LinkedList`.
- The last node has a null reference as there's no next node.
- All nodes in a `LinkedList` aren't stored in a contiguous memory location.

Based on the technique used to link the nodes of a `LinkedList`, we can categorize them into the following types:

- Singly Linked List
- Doubly Linked List
- Circular Linked List

Let's explore each of these types in detail.

Understanding a Singly Linked List

A Singly Linked List has a node containing the data and, at most, one reference pointing to the next node. If we try to represent a Singly Linked List in a diagram to make you understand it, this is what it looks like:

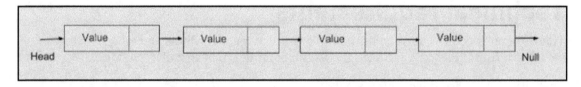

Let's implement a Singly Linked List to understand it further:

```
class LinkyList<E> {
    private var size = 0
    private var head: Node<E>? = null
    private var tail: Node<E>? = null
```

```
        private inner class Node<E> constructor(internal var element: E,
    internal var next: Node<E>?)
    }
```

The preceding snippet isn't the full implementation of a Singly Linked List. It's just a template of what the data structure looks like. We'll keep on adding multiple methods to perform different operations. A few points to remember from the preceding snippet are as follows:

- The class name is modified to `LinkyList` just to differentiate it from the name of the data structure, `LinkedList`. You can give it any name you want.
- As we call every element of `LinkedList` as `Node`, we created a private inner class called `Node`. This isn't visible to the outer world as the caller really doesn't care how we implemented it. The only thing they care about is their data, which will be exposed through an API.
- The first and the last node are called `head` and `tail` respectively. They're declared as nullable types, as they can have `null` values when the `LinkedList` is empty.
- The Node class doesn't have any default constructor because, to construct one node, we need both the element and the next node.

Operations on a Singly Linked List

The following operations can be done in a `LinkedList`:

- Inserting a node
- Fetching a node value
- Updating a node
- Deleting a node
- Searching for an element

We'll understand each of these operations thoroughly and, as we go ahead with examples, our `LinkedList` implementation will keep getting filled. In the end, we'll have a final and concrete implementation of a `LinkedList`.

Inserting a node in a Singly Linked List

Inserting a node can be dependent upon the position where we want to insert it. The following are a few of them:

- Inserting a node at the 0th index
- Inserting a node at the last index
- Inserting a node at a given index

For these preceding cases, we can define several public APIs such as `addFirst(element: E)`, `addLast(element: E)`, `add(element: E)`, and `add(index: Int, element: E)`. The snippets from below sections are these APIs with their implementation.

Inserting a node at the 0th index

To insert a node at the 0th index, we need to follow these steps:

1. Get the reference of the node at the 0th index.
2. Create a node with the element and the reference we got in step 1.
3. Make the newly created node `head` (0th node).

This is the way it looks graphically:

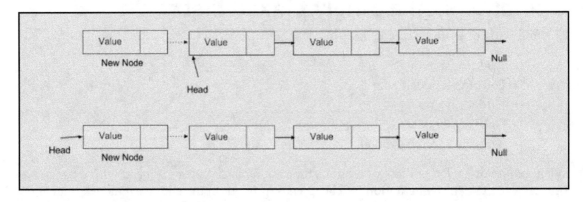

Here's the snippet that does this job:

```
fun addFirst(element: E) {
    val h = head
    val newNode = Node<E>(element, h)
    head = newNode
    if (h == null) {
        tail = newNode
```

```
    }
        size++
    }
```

 head is the node representing the 0th index of LinkedList.

Inserting a node at the last index

We can insert a node at the last index of LinkedList via the following steps:

1. Get the reference of the node at last index.
2. Create a node with the element and null.
3. Make the newly created node tail (last node).
4. Connect the node we got in step 1 with the new node.

This is the way it looks when represented in a diagram:

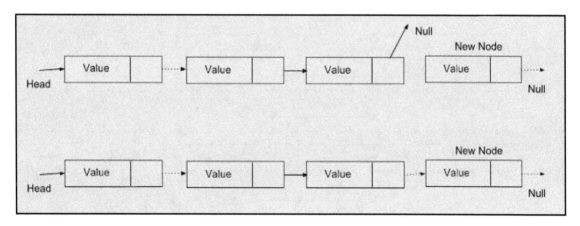

Here is the snippet that does this job:

```
fun addLast(element: E) {
    val t = tail
    val newNode = Node<E>(element, null)
    tail = newNode
    if (t == null) {
        head = newNode
    } else {
        t.next = newNode
```

```
        }
        size++
    }
```

  tail is the node representing the last `index` of `LinkedList`.

Inserting a node at a given index

We can insert a node at a given `index` of `LinkedList` via the following steps:

1. Get the reference of the node at the `index` - 1 position.
2. Create a node with the element and reference (that refers to the node at the given n^{th} index).
3. Make the newly created node as the next of the node at `index` - 1 position.

This is the way it looks when represented in a diagram:

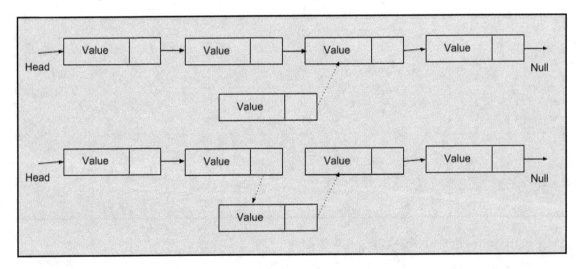

Here is the snippet that does this job:

```
fun add(index: Int, element: E) {
    validatePositionIndex(index)
    if (index == 0) linkHead(element)
    else {
        var x = head
        val prevIndex = index - 1
```

```
        for (i in 0 until prevIndex) {
            x = x!!.next
        }
        val next = x!!.next
        val newNode = Node(element, next)
        x.next = newNode
        size++
    }
}
```

Note that, before adding the element to the given index, we're first checking whether the index passed is a valid one or not. The following snippet does this validation:

```
private fun validatePositionIndex(index: Int) {
    if (index < 0 || index > size)
        throw IndexOutOfBoundsException(outOfBoundsMsg(index))
}

private fun outOfBoundsMsg(index: Int): String {
    return "Index: $index, Size: $size"
}
```

 Instead of having the code in add(), we created validatePositionIndex() and outOfBoundsMsg() as separate methods, because there are many more APIs in LinkedList that may need to reuse these two methods.

Fetching a node value from a Singly Linked List

Like insertion, fetching can also be dependent on the position of the node whose value we want to fetch. The following are a few of them:

- Fetching the first node value
- Fetching the last node value
- Fetching the value of a node at a given index

For these preceding cases, we can define several public APIs such as getFirst(), getLast(), and get(index: Int). The snippets from below sections are these APIs with their implementations.

Fetching a value from the first or last node

As a `first` and `last` node is already stored by `LinkedList`, we just need to return those as follows:

```
fun getFirst() = head?.element
fun getLast() = tail?.element
```

Fetching the value of a node at a given index

For nodes, except the first or last, we need to traverse till the given index to fetch the value. Here is the snippet for that:

```
fun get(index: Int): E {
    validateElementIndex(index)
    var x = head
    for (i in 0 until index) {
        x = x!!.next
    }
    return x!!.element
}
```

Note that, before getting the element from the given index, we're first checking whether the index passed is a valid one or not. The following snippet does this validation:

```
private fun validateElementIndex(index: Int) {
    if (index < 0 || index >= size)
        throw IndexOutOfBoundsException(outOfBoundsMsg(index))
}
```

Note, we have created another validation method called `validateElementIndex` in addition to `validatePositionIndex`. These two methods have different use cases, `validateElementIndex` should be used for doing any operation on an existing node, where as `validatePositionIndex` should be used for adding a new node. And the reason is, if the size of the list is 0 and the index it is asked to operate is also 0, then except add operation, all other operations (set, get, remove) should fail.

Updating a node from a Singly Linked List

Updating a node can also be exposed in many public APIs. Let's see how it looks when we want to update a node when index is given:

```
fun set(index: Int, element: E): E {
    validateElementIndex(index)
    var x = head
    for (i in 0 until index) {
        x = x!!.next
    }
    val oldVal = x!!.element
    x.element = element
    return oldVal
}
```

Deleting a node from a Singly Linked List

Deleting a node from a `LinkedList` can be done with APIs such as `remove(element: E)`, `remove(index: Int)`, `removeFirst()`, `removeLast()`, and `clear()`.

Removing the first and last node of a LinkedList

Removing the first node can be done via the following steps:

1. Get the next node of `head`.
2. Assign null to `head`.
3. Assign the node from step 1 to `head`.

Here is the code:

```
fun removeFirst() {
    head ? .let {
        val next = it.next
        it.next = null
        head = next
        if (next == null) {
            tail = null
        }
        size--
    }
}
```

Similarly, the code for removing the last node is as follows:

```
fun removeLast() {
    tail ? .let {
        val prev = getPrevious(it)
        tail = prev
        if (prev == null) {
            head = null
        } else {
            prev.next = null
        }
        size--
    }
}

private fun getPrevious(node: Node<E>): Node<E> ? {
    if (head != null && node == head) return null
    var curr = head
    while (curr != null) {
        if (curr.next == node) {
            return curr
        }
        curr = curr.next
    }
    return null
}
```

Removing the node based on its value

To remove a node as per its value, we need to follow these steps:

1. Traverse each node from head
2. Check the value of each node and compare it with the input
3. If it matches a particular node, then get the next and previous node of that node.
4. Connect both of the nodes from step 3.
5. Nullify the node that had the same value as the input.

Here is the code:

```
fun remove(element: E): Boolean {
    var curr = head
    while (curr != null) {
        if (curr.element == element) {
            unlink(curr)
            return true
        }
```

```
            curr = curr.next
        }
        return false
    }

    private fun unlink(curr: Node<E>): E {
        val element = curr.element
        val next = curr.next
        val prev = getPrevious(curr)
        if (prev == null) {
            head = next
        } else {
            prev.next = next
            curr.next = null
        }
        if (next == null) {
            prev ? .next = null
            tail = prev
        } else {
            prev ? .next = next
            curr.next = null
        }
        size--
        return element
    }
```

Removing the node at a particular index

This method uses the same `unlink` method defined in the previous section:

```
    fun remove(index: Int): E {
        validateElementIndex(index)
        return unlink(node(index))
    }
```

Clearing the LinkedList

This is how you can clear all of the elements of a `LinkedList` and make it empty:

```
    fun clear() {
        var x = head
        while (x != null) {
            val next = x.next
            x.next = null
            x = next
        }
        tail = null
```

```
        head = tail
        size = 0
    }
```

Searching for an element in a Singly Linked List

Searching for a value from a Singly Linked List can be done as follows:

```
fun indexOf(element: E): Int {
    var index = 0
    var x = head
    while (x != null) {
        if (element == x.element)
            return index
        index++
        x = x.next
    }
    return -1
}
```

As Kotlin provides a nice way to overload any operator, we can utilize that feature here by overloading the contains operator. Here is the code:

```
operator fun contains(element: E) = indexOf(element) != -1
```

This helps us to write code, as follows:

```
val linkyList = LinkyList<String>()
linkyList.add("Kotlin")
linkyList.add("Java")
linkyList.add("C#")
linkyList.add("C")
linkyList.add("C++")

println("JavaScript" in linkyList)
println("Kotlin" in linkyList)
```

 The last two statements of the preceding snippet use the in operator, which internally calls the overloaded contains() method.

Understanding the Doubly Linked List

In many operations operated on a Singly Linked List, we've observed that, to get a previous node of any particular node, we need to traverse from the `head` of the `LinkedList`. This is a performance hit. Of course, we can ignore it if the `LinkedList` is small but, for Linked Lists that are big in size, the time taken to get the previous node is larger. To avoid this performance problem, we can simply store the previous node reference of every node in the same way we store the next node reference. This is what we call a Doubly Linked List.

We can represent it in a graphical way as follows:

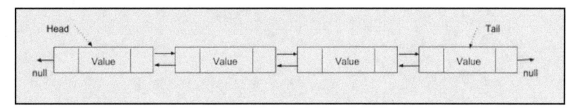

Like a Singly Linked List, we can perform all of those operations in a Doubly Linked List too. Moreover, all of those operations can be performed much faster because of the previous node's storage. Let's see the full implementation of a Doubly Linked List and then compare each operation with a Singly Linked List.

Here is the implementation:

```
class DoublyLinkyList<E> {
    private var size = 0
    private var head: Node<E>? = null
    private var tail: Node<E>? = null
    private inner class Node<E> constructor(internal var prev: Node<E>?,
internal var element: E, internal var next: Node<E>?)

    fun getFirst() = head?.element

    fun getLast() = tail?.element

    fun removeFirst() = unlinkHead()

    fun removeLast() = unlinkTail()
```

Here you start to add elements:

```
    fun addFirst(element: E) {
        linkHead(element)
    }
```

```
fun addLast(element: E) {
    linkTail(element)
}

fun add(element: E) {
    linkTail(element)
}

fun remove(element: E): Boolean {
    var curr = head
    while (curr != null) {
        if (curr.element == element) {
            unlink(curr)
            return true
        }
        curr = curr.next
    }
    return false
}

fun clear() {
    var x = head
    while (x != null) {
        val next = x.next
        x.next = null
        x.prev = null
        x = next
    }
    tail = null
    head = tail
    size = 0
}

fun size() = size

operator fun contains(element: E) = indexOf(element) != -1
```

We then validate the index values as follows:

```
fun get(index: Int): E {
    validateElementIndex(index)
    return node(index).element
}

fun set(index: Int, element: E): E {
    validateElementIndex(index)
    val x = node(index)
    val oldVal = x.element
```

```
        x.element = element
        return oldVal
    }

    fun add(index: Int, element: E) {
        validatePositionIndex(index)
        if (index == size) {
            linkTail(element)
        } else {
            linkBefore(element, node(index))
        }
    }
    fun remove(index: Int): E {
        validateElementIndex(index)
        return unlink(node(index))
    }

    fun indexOf(element: E): Int {
        var index = 0
        var x = head
        while (x != null) {
            if (element == x.element)
                return index
            index++
            x = x.next
        }
        return -1
    }
```

Then comes the linking of elements:

```
    private fun linkHead(element: E) {
    val h = head
    val newNode = Node<E>(null, element, h)
    head = newNode
    if (h == null) {
        tail = newNode
    } else {
        h.prev = newNode
    }
    size++
}

private fun linkTail(element: E) {
    val t = tail
    val newNode = Node<E>(t, element, null)
    tail = newNode
    if (t == null) {
```

```
        head = newNode
    } else {
        t.next = newNode
    }
    size++
}

private fun linkBefore(element: E, succ: Node<E>) {
    val pred = succ.prev
    val newNode = Node(pred, element, succ)
    succ.prev = newNode
    if (pred == null) {
        head = newNode
    } else {
        pred.next = newNode
    }
    size++
}
```

Once done, we unlink as follows:

```
private fun unlinkHead() {
head ? .let {
    val next = it.next
    it.next = null
    head = next
    if (next == null) {
        tail = null
    } else {
        next.prev = null
    }
    size--
}
}

private fun unlinkTail() {
    tail ? .let {
        val prev = it.prev
        it.prev = null
        tail = prev
        if (prev == null) {
            tail = null
        } else {
            prev.next = null
        }
        size--
    }
```

```
    }

    private fun unlink(curr: Node<E> ): E {
        val element = curr.element
        val next = curr.next
        val prev = curr.prev
        if (prev == null) {
            head = next
        } else {
            prev.next = next
            curr.prev = null
        }
        if (next == null) {
            tail = prev
        } else {
            next.prev = prev
            curr.next = null
        }
        size--
        return element
    }

    private fun node(index: Int): Node<E> {
        if (index < size shr 1) {
            var x = head
            for (i in 0 until index)
                x = x!!.next
            return x!!
        } else {
            var x = tail
            for (i in size - 1 downTo index + 1)
                x = x!!.prev
            return x!!
        }
    }
}
```

This is the final validation:

```
    private fun validateElementIndex(index: Int) {
        if (index < 0 || index >= size)
            throw IndexOutOfBoundsException(outOfBoundsMsg(index))
    }

    private fun validatePositionIndex(index: Int) {
        if (index < 0 && index > size)
            throw IndexOutOfBoundsException(outOfBoundsMsg(index))
    }
```

```
private fun outOfBoundsMsg(index: Int): String {
    return "Index: $index, Size: $size"
}
```

Many of the operations in a Doubly Linked List are done the same way as in a Singly Linked List. A few operations that have some differences are explained in the following sections.

Adding a node

The public API for adding a node as `head` (0th index) is `addFirst(element: E)`. But internally, it uses a private API called `linkHead(element: E)` to do the job. The differences between the API implementation of both data structures are mentioned as follows:

Singly Linked List	Doubly Linked List
The `linkHead` implementation is inline.	It's a separate private method.
A new node object is created as `Node<E>(element, h)`.	A new node is created as `Node<E>(null, element, h)`.
A previous `head` doesn't exist.	It's done as `h.prev = newNode`.

> The similar differences can be found when a node is added as the `tail` of the `LinkedList`. Check the `addLast()` API for more details.

A major difference we can find in the implementation of `add(index: Int, element: E)` is in a Singly Linked List, we traverse from `head` to get the previous node (check the `getPrevious(node: Node<E>)` API) of the given index whereas, in a Doubly Linked List, we avoid that as we already have a previous node reference.

Deleting a node

All `delete` operations are handled by APIs such as `remove(element: E)`, `remove(index: Int)` or `clear()`, and the private helper methods for these are `unlinkHead()`, `unlinkTail()`, and `unlink(curr: Node<E>)`.

The major difference we can find in these APIs is the way we handle previous node references in the case of a Doubly Linked List. As we store a reference of the previous node in each node, we need to nullify those in case of a Doubly Linked List. This step isn't required in a Singly Linked List. Check the mentioned implementations for more details.

Fetching a node

The API to fetch a node is node(index: Int). In a Singly Linked List, the node is fetched by traversing from head whereas, in a Doubly Linked List, it's optimized by checking that the given index is near to the head or tail. Based on that, we traverse either from the head or tail. Check the implementation for the detailed differences.

Understanding a Circular Linked List

In a Singly Linked List, the last node (tail) doesn't have a next node; similarly, in a Doubly Linked List, a head object's previous node reference and a tail object's next node reference are null. If we slightly modify these data structures to connect head and tail, then it can be called a **Circular Linked List**.

Graphically, it can be represented as follows:

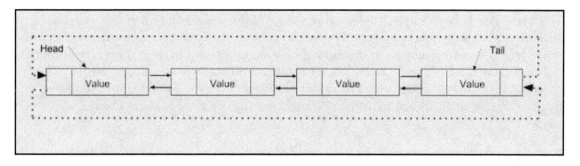

From the preceding diagram, it's clear that a Circular Linked List is nothing but a LinkedList whose **Head** (0th node) and **Tail** (last node) are connected. So the implementation of a Circular Linked List is the same as a Singly or Doubly Linked List with only one difference (connecting **Head** and **Tail**).

In the modern world, the topmost trending technology, Blockchain, is implemented with `LinkedList`. The following table explains this:

Operation	LinkedList	Array	Dynamic Array
Indexing	*O(n)*	*O(1)*	*O(1)*
Inserting/deleting at the beginning	*O(1)*	-	*O(n)*
Inserting/deleting at the end	*O(1)* - if the `tail` is known *O(n)* - if `tail` is unknown	-	*O(1)* - If not full *O(n)* - If full
Inserting/deleting in the middle	*O(n)*	-	*O(n)*

As the implementation is similar to a Singly and Doubly Linked List, we aren't covering the implementation here. Instead, it's a task for you—modify the Singly and Doubly Linked List to make a Circular Linked List.

Summary

A `LinkedList` is a very basic data structure and is commonly used to solve many computer science problems. In the old world, various operating systems' file management software was based on `LinkedList`.

So far, we've learned how to create a `LinkedList` and expose APIs to do operations on it. This is the best time to summarize the complexity of it compared to other discussed data structures such as arrays or vectors. We should choose `LinkedList` over arrays or vectors when we need more insertion or deletion operations compared to fetch (index) operation. If we need more fetch (index) operations, we should choose arrays or vectors over a `LinkedList`. This conclusion isn't final though. We should still consider space complexity. If space is more of a concern to us than time, then arrays or vectors always beat a `LinkedList`.

Now a query may arise, that, if we have decided to choose a `LinkedList`, then what should be its type? There's no hard and first rule for this, but we can choose based on a few factors like if more insertion and deletion of nodes happens in the middle of the list (except the first or last), then Doubly Linked List is preferable and if more operations happen at the end of the list,Circular Linked List is ideal as we don't need to traverse the entire list to reach the last node and then do the job.

To summarize when to choose what, the simplest solution is to check the pros and cons of all types of data structures explained in this chapter and pick which best suits the requirements.

The next chapter will help us understand the stacking and queues, their implementation and operation.

Questions

1. Write an API in linked list (LinkyList in this book) which adds all the elements of an array to the list.
2. Write the above API for doubly linked list (DoublyLinkyList in this book).
3. Write a snippet to link a node at head of a circular linked list.
4. Write a snippet to unlink a node from circular linked list.
5. Implement toString() method of circular linked list.

4
Understanding Stacks and Queues

In previous chapters, we covered linear data structures, such as an array, vector, and `LinkedList`. We were able to do any operation with any element. This chapter focuses mostly on abstracting those operations only to a certain element. This kind of abstraction can be looked at when we understand about data structures, such as stacks and queues. A stack is a data structure that allows us only to operate on the last element, whereas a queue allows us only to operate on the first and last element.

The following topics will be covered in this chapter:

- Understanding stacks
- Operations on stacks
- Implementation of stacks
- Understanding queues
- Operations on queues
- Implementation of queues
- Introducing circular queues
- Understanding **deque** (short for **double-ended queue**)

Technical requirements

There are no specific requirements here. To practice the algorithms and data structures we'll learn from this book, we need the Kotlin compiler to be installed on our PC.

The GitHub URL for the chapter is here:

```
https://github.com/PacktPublishing/Hands-On-Data-Structures-and-Algorithms-
with-Kotlin/tree/master/Chapter04
```

Understanding stacks

A stack is nothing but a simple linear data structure that abstracts all of the elements from the user except the last one. Imagine a situation where you have an array or a `LinkedList`, but you're only allowed to insert an element at the last index or delete only the last element. A linear data structure that can do this is called a **stack**. A stack can be implemented using any linear data structure, such as an array, vector, or `LinkedList`.

The following diagram shows a pictorial representation of a stack:

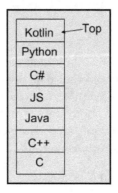

Operations on a stack

As mentioned earlier, a stack allows you to do an operation only with the last index. So, the operations possible on a stack are as follows:

- **Insertion**: This allows you to insert an element at last index (Top) of the stack. This operation is also called a **Push** operation.
- **Deletion**: This allows you to delete the element at last index (Top) of the stack. This operation is also called a **Pop** operation.

In addition to these primary operations, the stack can also allow a few secondary operations, such as the following:

- `Fetch`: Fetches the top of the stack, also called **Peek**
- `Size`: Returns the size of the stack
- `isEmpty`: Tells whether the stack is empty or not
- `isFull`: Tells whether the stack is full or not

If we closely observe the operations it allows us to do, we'll notice that the element that is being inserted (*Push*) last is deleted and (*Pop*) first. On the basis of these two primary operations (**Push** and **Pop**), a stack also can be called a **Last In, First Out** (**LIFO**) data structure.

The following diagram gives a pictorial representation of all stack operations:

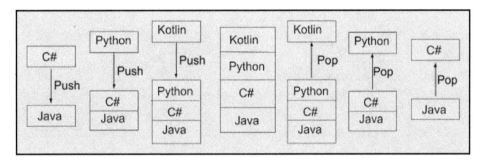

Implementing stacks

A stack can be implemented using any linear collection. In this section, we're going implement it using `Array` and `LinkedList`. Using an array, we can implement stacks of fixed and dynamic sizes.

Stacks with a fixed size

Although a fixed sized stack can be implemented using any linear data structure, we'll implement it using an array for simplicity.

In this implementation, as the stack size is fixed, the `push()` operation throws `StackOverflowException` after the stack is full. Similarly, the `pop()` operation throws `StackUnderflowException` when the stack is empty.

Here's is the implementation:

```
class FixedStack<E> {

    private val elements: Array<Any?>
    private var size = 0

    constructor(capacity: Int) {
        this.elements = arrayOfNulls(capacity)
```

```
    }

    fun push(element: E) {
        if (size == elements.size) {
            throw StackOverflowException()
        }
        elements[size++] = element
    }

    fun pop(): E {
        if (size == 0) throw StackUnderflowException()
        val index = --size
        val obj = elements[index]
        elements[index] = null
        return obj as E
    }

    fun peek() =try {
        elements[size - 1] as E
    } catch (e: IndexOutOfBoundsException) {
        throw StackUnderflowException();
    }

    fun isEmpty() = size == 0

    fun isFull() = size == elements.size
}

class StackUnderflowException: RuntimeException()

class StackOverflowException: RuntimeException()
```

Check the following descriptions to understand how a few of the previously mentioned operations work:

- push(): This checks whether the stack is full or not. If it's full, it throws StackOverflowException. Otherwise, it adds the given element into the backed-up array.
- pop(): This checks whether the stack is empty or not. If it's empty, it throws StackUnderflowException. Otherwise, it decrements the size property and returns the last element for the backed-up array.
- peek(): This returns the last element of the backed-up array without modifying the size property. It throws StackUnderflowException if the stack is empty.

Stacks with a dynamic size

A dynamic-sized stack can be implemented using an array, vector, or `LinkedList`. We'll do the implementation using an array. Here, the array grows when it's full. This growing nature and its implementation are similar to the way a vector's backed-up array grows.

Here is the implementation:

```
class Stack<E> {
    private val minCapacityIncrement = 12

    private var elements: Array<Any?>
    private var size = 0

    constructor() {
        this.elements = arrayOf()
    }

    constructor(initialCapacity: Int) {
        this.elements = arrayOfNulls(initialCapacity)
    }

    fun push(element: E) {
        if (size == elements.size) {
            val newArray = arrayOfNulls<Any>(size + if (size <
minCapacityIncrement / 2)
                minCapacityIncrement
            else
                size shr 1)
            System.arraycopy(elements, 0, newArray, 0, size)
            elements = newArray
        }
        elements[size++] = element
    }

    fun pop(): E {
        if (size == 0) throw StackUnderflowException()
        val index = --size
        val obj = elements[index]
        elements[index] = null
        return obj as E
    }

    fun peek() = try {
        elements[size - 1] as E
    } catch (e: IndexOutOfBoundsException) {
        throw StackUnderflowException();
```

```
        }
    }

    class StackUnderflowException : RuntimeException()
```

Here, all operations are the same as a fixed-sized stack except the `push()` one. The way `push()` works here is similar to the way `add()` works in a vector. It simply adds the given element at the last `index` of the array. And if the array is full, it creates a new array with an increased size. It then copies all existing elements into the new array and adds the element into the last `index` of the new array.

Stack implementation using a LinkedList

So far, we've implemented a stack using arrays. In this section, we'll see what a stack looks like when implemented using a `LinkedList`.

Here is the code:

```
class LinkedStack<E> {
    private var size = 0
    private var head: Node<E>? = null
    private var tail: Node<E>? = null

    private inner class Node<E> constructor(internal var prev: Node<E>?,
internal var element: E, internal var next: Node<E>?)

    fun push(element: E) {
        // Explained below
    }

    fun pop(): E {
        // Explained below
    }

    fun peek(): E {
        tail?.let {
            return it.element
        } ?: throw StackUnderflowException()
    }

    fun isEmpty() = size == 0
}
```

Although `LinkedStack` is based on a `LinkedList`, we don't expose any API to manipulate the data structure's elements, except the last node. The only two major APIs exposed are `push()` and `pop()`, which link a new node at the last node and unlinks the last node, respectively.

Pushing an element into the stack

Pushing an element to the stack is done using the `push()` APIs. If you observe closely, you'll notice that it's exactly the same as the `addLast` API of Doubly Linked List, which was explained in the `Chapter 3`, *Introducing Linked Lists*. Here is the code:

```
fun push(element: E) {
    val t = tail
    val newNode = Node<E>(t, element, null)
    tail = newNode
    if (t == null) {
        head = newNode
    } else {
        t.next = newNode
    }
    size++
}
```

Popping an element from the stack

Popping an element from the stack is done using the `pop()` API. If you observe closely, you'll notice that it's exactly the same as the `removeLast` API of Doubly Linked List. Here is the code:

```
fun pop(): E {
    tail?.let {
        val prev = it.prev
        it.prev = null
        tail = prev
        if (prev == null) {
            head = null
        } else {
            prev.next = null
        }
        size--
        return it.element
    } ?: throw StackUnderflowException()
}
```

One important point to note here is that, by removing all exposed methods except the `addLast` and `removeLast` APIs, Doubly Linked List can be converted into a stack.

Understanding a queue

Similar to a stack, a *queue* is also a simple linear data structure that abstracts all of the elements from the user except the first and last ones. The only difference between a stack and a queue is that a stack allows you to operate only on the last element, whereas a queue allows you to operate both on the first and last elements.

It can be implemented using any linear data structures, such as an array, vector, or `LinkedList`.

Graphically, we can represent it as follows:

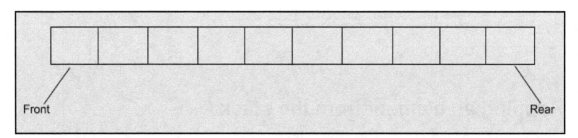

From the previous diagram, we can understand the following:

- **Front**: 0th index of the queue (backed up linear data structure)
- **Rear**: Last index of the queue (backed up linear data structure)

Operations on queues

Queues allow for operating only on the front and rear elements. Some basic operations are as follows:

- **Insertion**: This allows you to insert an element at the last index (rear) of the queue. This operation can also be termed **EnQueue**.
- **Deletion**: Allows you to delete an element from the first index (front) of the queue. This operation can also be termed **DeQueue**.

In addition to these two primary operations, a queue can also allow a few other operations, such as the following:

- `front()`: Returns the element at the front without mutating the queue
- `rear()`: Returns the element at the rear without mutating the queue
- `isEmpty()`: Tells whether a queue is empty or not
- `isFull()`: Tells whether a queue is full or not
- `size()`: Returns the size of the queue

If we closely observe the operations it allows us to do, we can notice that the element that's being enqueued first is dequeued first. On the basis of its primary operations (EnQueue and DeQueue), a queue also can be called a **First In, First Out (FIFO)** or **Last In, Last Out (LILO)** data structure.

Implementing a queue

A queue can be implemented using any linear data structure. Here, we'll implement a queue using an array, vector, and `LinkedList`. A fixed sized queue can be implemented using an array, whereas a dynamic sized queue can be implemented using a vector or `LinkedList`.

Queues with a fixed size

In this implementation, the queue size is fixed and the `enqueue()` operation throws `QueueOverflowException` after the queue is full.

Here is the implementation:

```
class FixedQueue<E> {

    private val elements: Array<Any?>
    private var size = 0

    constructor(capacity: Int) {
        this.elements = arrayOfNulls(capacity)
    }

    fun enqueue(element: E) {
        if (size == elements.size) {
            throw QueueOverflowException()
        }
```

```
            elements[size++] = element
    }

    fun dequeue(): E {
        if (size == 0) throw QueueUnderflowException()
        val oldVal = elements[0]
        elements[0] = null
        System.arraycopy(elements, 1, elements, 0, --size)
        return oldVal as E
    }

    fun front() = try {
        elements[0] as E
    } catch (e: IndexOutOfBoundsException) {
        throw QueueUnderflowException();
    }

    fun rear() = try {
        elements[size - 1] as E
    } catch (e: IndexOutOfBoundsException) {
        throw QueueUnderflowException();
    }

    fun isEmpty() = size == 0
}

class QueueUnderflowException : RuntimeException()

class QueueOverflowException : RuntimeException()
```

The following can be inferred from the previous code:

- `enqueue()`: This checks whether the queue is empty or not and adds the given element at the last index of the backed-up array if not full. It throws an exception if the queue is full.
- `dequeue()`: This checks whether the queue is empty or not and, if not empty caches the 0th element to a temporary variable and moves all of the elements from the first index to their previous index.
- `front()`: This returns the 0th element of the queue's backed-up array if not empty.
- `rear()`: This returns the last element of the queue's backed-up array if not empty.
- `isEmpty()`: This returns the size of the queue's backed-up array.

Queues with a dynamic size

This implementation is similar to the way a vector is implemented. Here, the queue never gets filled. Once it's filled and the user still tries to enqueue elements further, the backed-up array grows internally.

Here is the implementation:

```kotlin
class Queue<E> {
    private val minCapacityIncrement = 12

    private var elements: Array<Any?>
    private var size = 0

    constructor() {
        this.elements = arrayOf()
    }

    constructor(initialCapacity: Int) {
        this.elements = arrayOfNulls(initialCapacity)
    }

    fun enqueue(element: E) {
        // check below for it's implementation
    }

    fun dequeue(): E {
        if (size == 0) throw QueueUnderflowException()
        val oldVal = elements[0]
        elements[0] = null
        System.arraycopy(elements, 1, elements, 0, --size)
        return oldVal as E
    }

    fun front() = try {
        elements[0] as E
    } catch (e: IndexOutOfBoundsException) {
        throw QueueUnderflowException();
    }

    fun rear() = try {
        elements[size - 1] as E
    } catch (e: IndexOutOfBoundsException) {
        throw QueueUnderflowException();
    }

    fun isEmpty() = size == 0
```

```
    fun isFull() = size == elements.size
}
```

This implementation is almost the same as the previously discussed FixedQueue implementation. The major difference here is in the implementation of enqueue. Let's look at the following code:

```
fun enqueue(element: E) {
    if (size == elements.size) {
        val newArray = arrayOfNulls<Any>(size +
            if (size < minCapacityIncrement / 2)
                minCapacityIncrement
            else
                size shr 1)
        System.arraycopy(elements, 0, newArray, 0, size)
        elements = newArray
    }
    elements[size++] = element
}
```

In this implementation, the backed-up array grows when it's filled. This is a similar implementation to a vector's add API.

Queue implementation using LinkedList

So far we've implemented Queue using arrays. In this section, we'll see what a stack looks like when implemented using LinkedList.

Here is the code:

```
class LinkedQueue<E> {
    private var size = 0
    private var head: Node<E>? = null
    private var tail: Node<E>? = null

    private inner class Node<E> constructor(internal var prev: Node<E>?,
internal var element: E, internal var next: Node<E>?)

    fun enqueue(element: E) {
        val t = tail
        val newNode = Node<E>(t, element, null)
        tail = newNode
        if (t == null) { head = newNode } else { t.next = newNode }
        size++
    }
```

```
fun dequeue(): E {
    head?.let {
        val next = it.next
        it.next = null
        head = next
        if (next == null) { tail = null } else { next.prev = null }
        size--
        return it.element
    } ?: throw QueueUnderflowException()
}

fun front(): E {
    head?.let {
        return it.element
    } ?: throw QueueUnderflowException()
}

fun rear(): E {
    tail?.let {
        return it.element
    } ?: throw QueueUnderflowException()
}

fun isEmpty() = size == 0
}
```

Although `LinkedQueue` is based on `LinkedList`, we don't expose any API to manipulate the data structure's elements except the last node. The only two APIs exposed are `enqueue()` and `dequeue()`, which link a new node at the last node and unlink the first node, respectively. If you observe closely, you will find that the `enqueue` and `dequeue` APIs look exactly the same as `addLast` and `removeFirst` of Doubly Linked List, which we discussed in the `Chapter 3`, *Introducing Linked Lists*. In other words, we can say that, by removing all exposed methods except these two, Doubly Linked List can be converted into a queue.

Performance of a queue

The following table describes how a queue performs in different operations:

Operation	Fixed queue	Dynamic queue	Linked queue
enqueue()	O(1)	O(1)*	O(1)
dequeue()	O(1)#	O(1)#	O(1)
front()	O(1)	O(1)	O(1)

rear()	O(1)	O(1)	O(1)
isFull()	O(1)	NA	NA
isEmpty()	O(1)	O(1)	O(1)

The * enqueue() operation in a dynamic queue takes O(1) if it's not full. If the queue is full, then a new array is created and all old elements get copied. So, the complexity here isn't always O(1).

The # dequeue() operation in both fixed and dynamic queues takes an additional amount of time to move the elements to their corresponding previous index.

Introducing circular queues

So far we've looked into the way of implementing a queue using few linear data structures, such as an array and LinkedList. But there's a small performance improvement still needed in the earlier implementations. If you observe closely the performance table described in the previous section, you can see that the dequeue operation of a queue takes an additional amount of time to rearrange the elements of the array. We can improve this by implementing a **circular queue**.

We can define a circular queue as a queue that maintains two indices in it (front and rear) for doing enqueue and dequeue operations. In this case, enqueue is not always adding an element at the last index. Similarly, dequeue is not always removing an element from 0th index.

The following snippet shows what the circular queue looks like:

```
class CircularFixedQueue<E> {

    private val capacity: Int
    private var front = -1
    private var rear = -1
    private val elements: Array<Any?>

    constructor(capacity: Int) {
        this.capacity = capacity
        this.elements = arrayOfNulls(capacity)
    }

    fun enqueue(element: E) {
        // check below for implementation
    }
```

```
fun dequeue(): E {
    // check below for implementation
}
}
```

In addition to capacity and elements, here we can see two more properties called **front** and **rear**:

- `front`: This represents an index that will be used for the next `dequeue` operation.
- `rear`: This represents an index that will be used for the next `enqueue` operation.

Primary operations in a circular queue

Primary operations (`enqueue` and `dequeue`) of a circular queue aren't always operating on last index or 0th index. When the queue is created, both the front and rear aren't pointing to any valid index as the queue is empty. After the creation, based on the operation we perform on the queue, the front and rear values get changed.

The following snippet shows how the `enqueue` operation works:

```
fun enqueue(element: E) {
    if (isFull()) throw QueueOverflowException()
    rear = (rear + 1) % capacity
    elements[rear] = element
    if (front == -1) front = rear
}
```

Here, we increase the rear value by 1 to get the index where we need to insert the given element. As we can't keep on incrementing the rear value, a reminder is calculated with the capacity of the queue to make the *rear* value in the boundary.

The following snippet explains the way the operation works:

```
fun dequeue(): E {
    if (isEmpty()) throw QueueUnderflowException()
    val oldVal = elements[front]
    elements[front] = null
    if (front == rear) {
        front = -1
        rear = -1
    } else front = (front + 1) % capacity
    return oldVal as E
}
```

Here, we first remove the element present at the front index and then, based on the following condition, we act accordingly. If both front and rear have the same value, it means the queue is empty, and we reset their values to -1. If they are not the same, we just increment the front value for the next operation.

Secondary operations in a circular queue

Like other queues, we've a similar implementation for all secondary operations. The following code snippet explains the way they work:

```
fun front() = try {
    elements[front] as E
} catch (e: IndexOutOfBoundsException) {
    throw QueueUnderflowException();
}

fun rear() = try {
    elements[rear] as E
} catch (e: IndexOutOfBoundsException) {
    throw QueueUnderflowException();
}

fun isEmpty() = front == -1

fun isFull() = (rear + 1) % capacity == front
```

From the preceding code, we can understand the following:

- `front()`: Fetches the index represented by the `front` property
- `rear()`: Fetches the index represented by the `rear` property
- `isEmpty()`: Returns `true` if `front` doesn't point to any valid index
- `isFull()`: Returns `true` if `rear` value is pointing to the previous index of the front

Understanding deque – double-ended queue

Deque is a special queue where both primary operations (`enqueue` and `dequeue`) can be done from both the front and rear end. So, we can imagine it as a queue with additional APIs. The code looks similar to other queues with two additional operations. The upcoming section will discuss these additional operations.

Primary operations – deque

Instead of enqueue and dequeue, the APIs here are enqueueFront, enqueueRear, dequeueFront, and dequeueRear. In a usual queue, the enqueue operation happens at the rear end, so there is no need to discuss the enqueueRear API here. Similarly, the dequeueFront API is not discussed here.

The other two APIs look like the following:

```
fun enqueueFront(element: E) {
    if (size == elements.size) {
        val newArray = arrayOfNulls<Any>(size + if (size <
minCapacityIncrement / 2)
            minCapacityIncrement
        else
            size shr 1)
        System.arraycopy(elements, 0, newArray, 1, size)
        elements = newArray
    } else {
        System.arraycopy(elements, 0, elements, 1, size)
    }
    elements[0] = element
    size++
}
```

The enqueueFront() implementation is the same as a vector's add(index: Int) API by passing 0 as the input. This is explained in the following code:

```
fun dequeueRear(): E {
    if (size == 0) throw DequeUnderflowException()
    val oldVal = elements[--size]
    elements[size] = null
    return oldVal as E
}
```

The dequeueRear() operation implementation looks the same as a vector's remove(index: Int) API by passing 0 as the input.

 For full implementation of the deque, please check out our GitHub repository at https://github.com/PacktPublishing/Hands-On-Data-Structures-and-Algorithms-with-Kotlin/blob/master/Chapter04/Deque.kt .

Summary

In this chapter, we learnt that a stack is a simple linear data structure abstracting all elements from the user except the very last one.

A queue is one of the widely used data structures. Using a queue, we can solve many problems, such as distributing time among processors in a round-robin mechanism, job scheduling, a print queue in a printer, messaging systems, asynchronous applications, and so on. A queue uses the FIFO method to operate on its data. In addition to FIFO, a queue can also be represented as a LIFO or FCFS data structure.

If we've a scenario where the buffer is of a fixed size, then we should always go for fixed queue implementation, for example, a queue in a cinema theatre. Here, the seat count is 200, so we can create a buffer size of 200 and, as the people come in, we serve them in the FCFS manner until all 200 seats are full.

Whereas if you can serve as many people as come, then we can choose a dynamic queue. For example, devotees coming to a temple. The queue can grow as big as possible. Here, the queue gets enqueued and dequeued simultaneously. So, we might need to implement a thread-safe queue to solve this problem.

Questions

1. Implement a fixed-sized double-ended queue (`FixedDeque`).
2. Implement a dynamic-sized circular queue.
3. Imagine a situation where lots of people are standing in a queue to enter a temple and the queue gets enqueued by a group of people. Similarly, it gets dequeued by a group of people. So we need to have the `enqueue()` and `dequeue()` APIs to support collections instead of just a single element.
4. To enter into a temple, there are three queues and each queue is associated with a ticket system. All of these three queues get served based on their priority. The higher the ticket cost, the higher the priority they get served. Design such a kind of system using a queue that understands priority. The ticket prices are as follows:
    1. Free—the longer queue as more people opt for it
    2. ₹50—A bit shorter queue
    3. ₹100— The Shortest queue
5. Implement a queue that's thread safe.

Further reading

For more information about queues and other ways of implementing them, you can refer to the `java.util.Queue` interface and their implemented classes in Java's collection package. Some of the important implementations are `BlockingQueue`, `PriorityQueue`, `SynchronousQueue`, and so on.

Questions

1. Write an API to push all the elements of an array to a stack.
2. Write an API to enqueue all the elements of an array to a queue.
3. Write an API to pop a given number of elements from the stack.
4. Write an API to dequeue a given number of elements from the queue.
5. Write APIs called stackOf() and queueOf() which works similar to arrayOf().

5
Maps - Working with Key-value Pairs

Unlike arrays and vectors, which deal with collections of single elements, Map is a data structure that deals with collections of pairs. A pair is an entry in Map, which consists of a key and a value associated with that particular `key`. The `key` is an important factor of a Map when it comes to doing any operation on a Map.

In this chapter, we'll learn the following:

- Implementing hashing
- Implementing `HashMap`
- `ArrayMap` and some of its basics

Technical requirements

There are no specific requirements here. To practice the algorithms and data structures we'll learn from this book, we need the Kotlin compiler to be installed on our PC.

The GitHub URL for the chapter is here:

```
https://github.com/PacktPublishing/Hands-On-Data-Structures-and-Algorithms-
with-Kotlin/tree/master/Chapter05.
```

Introducing Map

A few important points to note about Map are:

- It's a data structure that maps keys to values.
- All keys in a Map should be unique. Using duplicate keys for any operation will lead to that operation being implemented on the earlier existing `key`.
- A `key` can be mapped to one value. The value can be an object or list of objects.
- Whether we should allow `null` as a `key` or not isn't firmly specified. Depending upon our requirements, we can implement a Map that either allows `null` as a `key`, or doesn't.
- Since Map doesn't deal with indexes, maintaining the order of the entries isn't guaranteed.
- The objects used as keys in any Map should ideally implement the `equals` and the `hashCode` methods. All operations on Map can be done using these methods.
- As keys are used for all operations in Map, we need to be very careful in choosing mutable data types as keys.

Operations in Map

Just as an index is used for operations with respect to data structures such as Array or Vector, `key` is used for operations with regard to Maps.

The following table explains the API differences between these two data structures:

Operation	Array or Vector	Map
Insertion	`add(index: Int)`	`put(key: K, value: V)`
Deletion	`remove(index: Int): E`	`remove(key: K): V`
Fetch	`get(index: Int): E`	`get(key: K): V`
Updation	`set(index: Int)`	`replace(key: K, value: V)`

As all operations of use a `key`, Map cannot follow a single rule for any operation, as keys can be of the `Any` type and can represent anything. For example, a `key` can be an Integer, a String, or a User. This will make all the operations perform slower, as Map can't address any entry directly. For example—in the case of *Array or Vector*, `any` operation is done using the direct address of that particular element, resulting in *O(1)* performance. But in Map, as index is not present, we can't address any entry directly, resulting in slower performance. To avoid this, Map converts the keys into a specific type to make it possible for direct addressing. For example, whether the `key` is a String or User, it gets converted to an `int`, which is used for addressing any entry directly. The conversion happens by applying an algorithm called **hashing**. So, before we proceed further with various types of Maps, we need to understand what hashing is and how to use it to convert a `key` of `Any` type into an integer.

Introducing hashing

To understand hashing, let's consider a small example where you want to store details of students in a Map, where `key` is the student ID and *value* is the student object. As student IDs can be alphanumeric, the number of possible keys is infinite. Now, in order to fetch a student's details from their ID, we first need to search the IDs and then fetch the details. It takes *O(n)* to do the required task.

To make it faster, we can slightly change the approach by storing the entries. Instead of storing each entry individually, we can store them based on the first character of the ID. If a student has an ID that starts with *a*, then we store their details in the 0th index, *b* in the first index, *c* in the second index, and so on. By following this approach, we can make our Map operate *26 times faster* than the earlier approach.

If we look closely, we should be able to notice that in the latter approach, we tried to map an infinite possible number of keys to a finite possible number of indices (26, in this example). This method of mapping a dataset of infinite possible size to a finite dataset is called **hashing**.

In simple terms, we can define hashing as an algorithm that maps data of arbitrary size to data of a fixed size. The result (that is, fixe-size data) from a hashing algorithm is called a **hash code** or **hash value**.

Benefits of hashing

In the preceding example, we found that by applying hashing, we made our algorithm performance 26 times faster than the non-hashed algorithm. But that is not all we can do – we can still optimize our hashing technique to make it even faster. For example, instead of generating the index from the first character of the student ID, we can generate the index from the whole student ID. As all IDs are unique, we can generate unique indices for each student, resulting in each index representing only one student. By doing this, we can make our algorithm perform in *O(1)*.

So, we can conclude that by using the hashing technique, we can perform any operation (`insert`, `fetch`, and so on) in a faster way (that is, *O(1)* complexity).

The hash function

The `hash` function is essentially a normal function that takes `key` as an input and generates the hash value out of it. The following code shows how this looks for the aforementioned example:

```
fun hashCodeFromId(studentId: String) = studentId[0].toUpperCase() - 'A'
```

The preceding snippet shows a `hash` function that takes a student *ID* (`String` type) as input and calculates the hash value (of the `int` type) from its first character. The results of the preceding a `hash` function should be `Art0001 -> 0`, `axe002 -> 0`, `Bml003 -> 1`, `bxt004 -> 1`, and so on.

Hash collision

The preceding snippet is shown just as an example. It is not recommended to implement a `hash` function in that way because it has a high possibility of generating the same hash values for different keys. For example, the preceding `hash` function generates 0 as the hash value for all keys that start with *a* or *A*. As hash values for different keys can be the same, we call this a **hash collision**.

It is highly recommended to create your `hash` function in such a way that the hash value generated should have as few collision as possible.

Fixing collisions with chaining

As we found that multiple keys can have same hash value, we need to support multiple entries to be stored in a single bucket. To make this possible, the entries with the same hash value are chained among themselves using `LinkedList`. To understand this better, let's consider the following example.

In a school, there are *n* students (for example, 250) and we need to store all of their details with `student_id` as the `key` and student details as the value. We have the following cases:

- **Base case**: If the `hash` function is able to generate n unique hash values (250 here), then there is no hash collision and of course no chaining. Each student will get a unique bucket. As a result, the search will be in *O(1)* and delete will also be in *O(1)*.
- **Average case**: If the `hash` function generates a hash value that collides with other keys equally among `student_id` instances (for example, *n/10 students - 1* hash value), then there are 10 buckets, each containing a chain of n/10 students (25 here). As a result, the search will be *n/10* times (25 times) slower than the best case.
- **Worst case**: If the `hash` function generates the same hash value for all `student_id` instances, then all students will be chained under a single bucket, so both search and `delete` operations will be of *O(n)*.

Implementing HashMap

So far, we have seen how a Map works internally. In this section, we'll try to create a simple Map and understand how the preceding topics can be implemented. Instead of looking at the whole implementation in a single place, we'll try to understand it chunk by chunk. For the full implementation, please visit this book's GitHub repository.

A template of the HashMap class

Since the implementation is based on hashing, we named it `HashMap`. There is nothing strict about the naming though. The following is the template code for our `HashMap`:

```
class HashMap<K, V> {
    private val minCapacity = 1 shl 4
    private val maxCapacity = 1 shl 30
    private var table: Array<Node<K, V>?>
    var size = 0
```

```
        private set

    constructor() {
        this.table = arrayOfNulls(minCapacity)
    }

    constructor(capacity: Int) {
        if (capacity < 0) throw IllegalArgumentException("Invalid Capacity:
$capacity")
        val finalCapacity = when {
            capacity < minCapacity -> minCapacity
            capacity > maxCapacity -> maxCapacity
            else -> fetchNearestCapacity(capacity)
        }
        this.table = arrayOfNulls(finalCapacity)
    }
    // .... Further Code will be explained in the following section
}
```

The preceding code snippet is not the full implementation of `HashMap`. It just gives you an initial feel of how it looks and how we can construct `HashMap` using its multiple constructors. Before we see any further implementation, let's first understand what is present in the preceding code snippet, as follows:

- **Capacity**: Two properties, `minCapacity` and `maxCapacity`, are usually used to define the minimum and maximum number of buckets that `HashMap` can have. Please note that `minCapacity` is initialized with 2^4 and `maxCapacity` is initialized with 2^{30}. The reason behind choosing their values as a *power of 2* is to make the bucket index calculation a bit easier with bitwise operators.
- **Table**: The `table` property clearly indicates that `HashMap` is nothing but a simple array of *nodes*. A **node** is nothing but an inner class similar to what we saw in the `LinkedList` data structure. We'll discuss it later.
- **Size**: The `size` property defines the number of entries (key-value pairs) present in `HashMap` at any particular time. Note that this has a private setter, which means we can't set any value to it from outside as it is completely dependent upon the `put` and `remove` operations that we do on `HashMap`.
- **Constructors**: There can be any number of constructors, depending upon the way you want to design your data structure. Here, we have two constructors. The zero argument creates an array with the minimum bucket size (`minCapacity`). The other constructor, which takes capacity as an argument, creates an array with a bucket size in the range of `minCapacity` and `maxCapacity`. Note that if the capacity passed is not a power of two, we get the nearest capacity from the `fetchNearestCapacity` method.

minCapacity and maxCapacity can also be used to resize HashMap when its size exceeds a threshold limit. But since we are discussing an implementation of a fixed sized HashMap, we use these properties only for initializing the array while constructing HashMap.

The Node class of HashMap

As we saw in the preceding section, HashMap is nothing but an array of *nodes*. Let's see how it is implemented, as follows:

```
private class Node<K, V>(
    val hash: Int,
    val key: K,
    var value: V,
    var next: Node<K, V>?) {

    override fun toString() = "$key=$value"

    override fun hashCode() = (key?.hashCode() ?: 0).xor(value?.hashCode()
?: 0)

    override fun equals(other: Any?): Boolean {
        if (other === this) return true
        if (other is Node<*, *> && this.key == other.key && this.value ==
other.value) return true
        return false
    }
}
```

A few points to note in the preceding code snippet are as follows:

- Node is a simple class with a hash, a key, a value, and a reference to the next node.
- This is similar to the Node class defined in the LinkedList class.
- Each index (bucket) of the array (table) holds a reference to this class representing the first (head) of the LinkedList that corresponds to that particular bucket.

The hash function of HashMap

As we have already discussed what a `hash` function is and how can we generate a hash value in the preceding section, let's see how it looks in the `HashMap` class here:

```
private fun hash(key: K): Int {
    val h = key?.hashCode() ?: 0
    return h xor (h ushr 16)
}
```

In the earlier example of a `hash` function, we have tried to create a hash value of a `String`. But in this case, since `HashMap` is a generic class, we have to create a `hash` function that can generate hash value from the `Any` type. This is the reason we are using `hashCode` to achieve this. Note that in this `hash` function, we are also trying to do some bit calculation to make `hash` more unique and reduce the possibility of a hash collision as much as possible.

 There is no hard and fast rule for creating a `hash` function. You can create it in your own way.

Operations on HashMap

So far, we have created all the infrastructure required for `HashMap`. Let's now create the real APIs of `HashMap` and understand how we can do various operations on `HashMap`. In the previous section, we understood how to create `HashMap`; let's now look at other operations in this section.

Three major operations we are going to discuss here are as follows:

- Putting a key-value pair into `HashMap`
- Getting a value from `HashMap`
- Removing a key-value pair from `HashMap`

Before we jump into understanding all the aforementioned operations, let's first try to understand a common task we need to do to complete any of the preceding three operations.

Determining the bucket from the key

Whether we try to put an entry or get an entry, any operation on HashMap should go with this task. For example, we want to fetch a value from HashMap using a given key. To do that, we have to first find which bucket the given key is representing. Once we get the required bucket index, we now do a linear search over LinkedList to get the value.

We can find the bucket index based on the way HashMap is implemented. Here are a few examples:

1. Let's say we are dealing with the String type as our key, and our hash function is generating hash values as per the first character of the key (as explained in the earlier section). In this case, we know that there could be a bucket size of 26. The 0th bucket has all the entries with keys starting from 'A', and so on. Now, to determine the bucket index, we can write our logic as follows:

   ```
   fun getBucketIndex(key: String) = key[0].toUpperCase() - 'A'
   ```

    In the preceding example, we have ignored all special characters, digits, and lower case letters to make the explanation simpler. In a real implementation, we should not do it this way.

2. Let's say we want to implement HashMap, whose size is always fixed at 100 (for example). Now, the bucket index can be calculated as follows:

   ```
   fun getBucketIndex(key: K) = key.hashCode() % 100
   ```

   As the modulus operator guarantees a value of less than 100, we are safe to use this in a real implementation.

3. This is the implementation we are going to use in our HashMap implementation:

   ```
   fun getBucketIndex(key: K) {
       val hash = hash(key)
       val lastIndex = table.size - 1
       val bucketIndex = lastIndex and hash
   }
   ```

Like the modulus operator, the bitwise AND operator also guarantees a value less than or equal to the last index of the table.

With various methods of bucket index calculation in mind, now let's see how can we implement the real APIs outlined in this section.

Putting a key-value pair into the HashMap

This operation can be exposed in two APIs, as follows:

```
fun put(key: K, value: V) {
    putVal(key, value)
}

fun putIfAbsent(key: K, value: V) {
    putVal(key, value, true)
}
```

Both of the preceding APIs insert a key-value pair into HashMap. But the later does it only if there is no entry already available with the given key. As we can see, both of these APIs call an internal method, putVal, to do their job. Let's see how that method looks in the following code:

```
private fun putVal(key: K, value: V, onlyIfAbsent: Boolean = false) {
    val hash = hash(key)
    val n = table.size
    val index = (n - 1) and hash
    var first = table[index]
    if (first == null) {
        table[index] = Node(hash, key, value, null)
        ++size
    } else {
        var node: Node<K, V>?
        var k = first.key
        if (first.hash == hash
          && (k === key || k == key)
          && !onlyIfAbsent)
            first.value = value
        else {
            while(true) {
                node = first!!.next
                if (node == null) {
                    first.next = Node(hash, key, value, null)
                    break
                }
                k = node.key
                if (node.hash == hash
                  && (k === key || k == key)
                  && !onlyIfAbsent) {
                    node.value = value
                    break
                }
                first = node
```

```
        }
      }
    }
  }
```

Let's try to understand the preceding method's logic step by step:

1. The first three lines of the snippet calculate the bucket index. This is already discussed in the *Determining the bucket from the key* section.

2. Then, we get the head node of `LinkedList` associated with the bucket index calculated in the preceding step.

3. Next, check whether the head of `LinkedList` is null or not. If `null`, then it clearly indicates that there were no entries in `HashMap` with the given `key`. So, create a new `Node` and assign it to the bucket index.

4. If the head of `LinkedList` is not `null`, then get its `key` and `hash` to compare with the input. If they're the same, we've found the required node, so assign the head's value with input value.

5. If the details of the head node are not the same as the input details, then do a linear search over all the nodes until we find our required node. This is the same as searching something in `LinkedList` explained in the `chapter 3`, *Introducing Linked Lists*.

6. If we find the required node in *step 5*, then assign the node's value with the input value (as in *step 4*).

7. If we don't find the required node in *step 5* and reach the last node, then create a new `Node` with the input details and attach it, as the next node, to the last node.

 Put simply, we can say that this operation is finding the bucket index and then doing a `LinkedList` search until you find the required node to put the value.

Getting a value from HashMap

This operation can be exposed as the following API:

```
fun get(key: K): V? {
    val e = getNode(hash(key), key)
    return if (e == null) null else e.value
}
```

Note that the public `get` API uses a private method called `getNode` and returns the value from the node produced by the `getNode` method. If the required node is not found, then the `get` API returns `null`. Let's look at the private method `getNode`:

```
private fun getNode(hash: Int, key: K): Node<K, V>? {
    val n = table.size
    if (n > 0) {
        val first = table[(n - 1) and hash]
        if (first != null) {
            if (first.hash == hash) { // Checking the 1st node
                val k = first.key
                if (k === key || k == key) return first
            }
            var e = first.next ?: return null
            do {
                if (e.hash == hash && e.key === key || e.key == key)
return e
            } while (e.next != null)
        }
    }
    return null
}
```

Let's try to understand the preceding method's logic step by step:

1. Check whether the bucket size is 0 or more. If it is 0, then return `null` as there is no bucket created yet.
2. If buckets are present, then calculate the required bucket index and get the head node of `LinkedList` associated with the calculated bucket index.
3. If the head of `LinkedList` is not `null`, then get its `key` and `hash` to compare with the input. If they're the same, we've found the required node, so return it.
4. If the details of the head node are not the same as the input details, then do a linear search over all the nodes until we find our required node or reach the last node.
5. If the node found has same details as the input, return it. Otherwise, if we reached the last index, then return `null`.

Removing a key-value pair from HashMap

This operation can be exposed as `remove(key:K) : V?`. Here is the code:

```
fun remove(key: K): V? {
    val hash = hash(key)
    val n = table.size
```

```
val index = (n - 1) and hash
var first = table[index]
if (n > 0 && first != null) {
    var node: Node<K, V>? = null
    var k = first.key
    if (first.hash == hash && (key === k || key == k)) node = first
    else {
        var nextNode = first.next
        if (nextNode != null) {
            do {
                k = nextNode!!.key
                if (nextNode.hash == hash && (key === k || key == k)) {
                    node = nextNode
                    break
                }
                first = nextNode
                nextNode = nextNode.next
            } while(nextNode != null)
        }
    }
    if (node != null) {
        if (node == first) table[index] = node.next
        else first!!.next = node.next
        --size
        return node.value
    }
}
return null
}
```

Like other APIs, let's try to understand this in a step-by-step manner:

1. We calculate the bucket index and get the `head` node.

2. If the head node is not `null`, then check its details with the input's. If they're the same, remove the head and make its next node the head of `LinkedList` of that particular bucket. The snippet from the preceding code block for this step is as follows:

   ```
   if (first.hash == hash && (key === k || key == k)) node = first
   if (node == first) table[index] = node.next
   ```

3. If the details of the head node are not the same as the input's, do a linear search until we find the required node, then remove it.

All these operations that we read on `HashMap` are similar to the `LinkedList` operations we read in an earlier chapter. The only difference here is we need to find the bucket index first, and then do the `LinkedList` operation.

Implementing ArrayMap

In the previous section, we have seen how to implement `HashMap`. Though it is one of the best data structures for key-value pairs, we still can learn other similar data structures that have slightly different approaches to achieving the same goal. `ArrayMap` is one of them. Before we go ahead with the implementation of `ArrayMap`, let's first understand the difference between this and `HashMap` to understand why we even need `ArrayMap` and where can we use it:

- `HashMap` uses Nodes to store key-value pairs. So, in addition to the actual data, it also allocates memory for the reference to the next node, whereas `ArrayMap` doesn't need this.
- To avoid hash collisions, `HashMap` creates a larger array even though most of the indexes could be empty, whereas `ArrayMap` doesn't require this.

We'll understand more about the aforementioned points in later parts of this chapter.

Internal data structure of ArrayMap

`ArrayMap` is basically a wrapper of two arrays, one storing the hash values and the other storing the keys and values. The following diagram gives you a brief idea of how it stores the data:

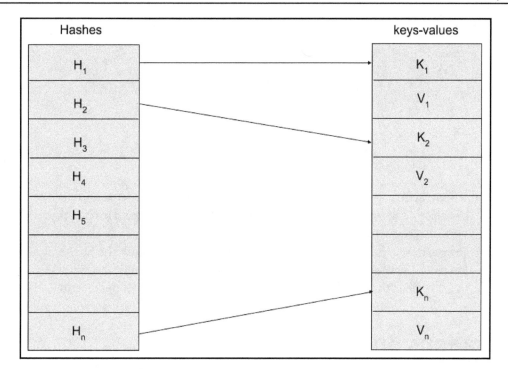

As you can see, `ArrayMap` is completely based on arrays, which is why it is named as such. In the following sections, we'll learn how these two arrays are used in `ArrayMap`. Like `HashMap`, this section will also explain the implementation of `ArrayMap` chunk by chunk.

A template of the ArrayMap class

The following code snippet has information about how `ArrayMap` is declared, what properties it has, and its constructors:

```
class ArrayMap<K, V> constructor(capacity: Int = 0) {
    private lateinit var hashes: IntArray
    private lateinit var array: Array<Any?>

    var size = 0
        private set

    init {
        if(capacity <= 0) {
            hashes = IntArray(0)
            array = arrayOf()
        } else allocArrays(capacity)
```

```
    }

    private fun allocArrays(size: Int) {
        hashes = IntArray(size)
        array = arrayOfNulls(size shl 1) // size * 2
    }

    // .... Further Code will be explained in the following section
}
```

Let's understand what the preceding code does:

- **Constructors**: It has two constructors—an empty constructor and another with capacity as its argument. The default capacity is 0. As per the capacity, it allocates the arrays.
- **Properties**: It has two arrays—an array of integers to store the hash values of keys, and another array of type `Any`, which stores `key` and value consecutively. So, it is clear that a data array is always twice the size of a hash array.

Operations on ArrayMap

So far, we have created all the infrastructure required for `ArrayMap`. Let's now create the real APIs of `ArrayMap` and understand how we can do various operations on `ArrayMap`. In the previous section, we have already examined both ways to create `ArrayMap`, so let's now look at other operations in this section.

Three major operations we are going to discuss here are as follows:

1. Putting a key-value pair into `ArrayMap`
2. Getting a value from `ArrayMap`
3. Removing a key-value pair from `ArrayMap`

Putting a key-value pair into ArrayMap

Here is the way it is implemented:

```
fun put(key: K, value: V): V? {
    val hash: Int
    var index: Int
    if (key == null) {
        hash = 0
        index = indexOfNull()
```

```
    } else {
        hash = key.hashCode()
        index = indexOf(key)
    }
    if (index >= 0) {
        // key-value pair already present
        index = (index shl 1) + 1
        val old = array[index] as V
        array[index] = value
        return old
    }

    index = index.inv()
    if (size >= hashes.size) {
        val newSize = if (size < 4) 4 else size + (size shr 1)
        val tempHashes = hashes
        val tempArray = array
        allocArrays(newSize)

        System.arraycopy(tempHashes, 0, hashes, 0, tempHashes.size)
        System.arraycopy(tempArray, 0, array, 0, tempArray.size)
    }

    if (index < size) {
        System.arraycopy(hashes, index, hashes, index + 1, size - index)
        System.arraycopy(array, index shl 1, array, (index + 1) shl 1,
(size - index) shl 1)
    }

    hashes[index] = hash
    array[index shl 1] = key
    array[(index shl 1) + 1] = value
    size++
    return null
}
```

Let's try to understand the preceding method's logic step by step:

1. First, we check whether the key is `null` or not. As per its value, we get the hash value and its index. If `key` is present already, then the index will be a positive value; otherwise, we'll get a negative one.

 Both `indexOfNull()` and `indexOf(key)` will be discussed later.

2. Check whether the index fetched in the previous step is a positive or negative number. If positive, it shows that the given `key` is already present in `ArrayMap`, hence it's a `replace` operation. So, calculate the index of the *value* in the data array and assign it with *new value*.

 If the `index` of a `hash` h_1 is *i*, then *index of key* = 2 * i and *index of value* = (2 * i) + 1.

3. If the index fetched in *step 1* is negative, it indicates that the given is not present in `ArrayMap`, so we need to enter a completely new entry.

4. Check whether `ArrayMap` is full or has space for the new entry. If it's full, then refer the existing arrays (both data and hash array) by new variables (for future use) and allocate larger arrays to both the data and hash arrays. Once the new arrays are created, copy the existing `hashes` and data to the newly allocated arrays.

5. By the end of *step 4*, we now have space for a new entry. Check whether the entry should be added to the end of the array or somewhere in the middle.

6. If we need to put the entry in the middle of the array, then first we need to vacate the space by shifting the later indexes by 1 (hash array) and 2 (data array) positions forward. For example, if the size of `ArrayMap` is 10, but the index's new entry should go in 4, then the fourth index of the hash array and the indexes 8 and 9 of the data array should be empty. To do this, we need to shift all the values (from index 4) of the hash array by 1 index position, and all the values (from index 8) of the data array by 2 indexes forward.

7. Now, we have empty space for the new entry. Assign `hash`, `key`, and `value` to their respective indexes and increment the `ArrayMap` size by 1.

Getting a value from ArrayMap

Here is the way it is implemented:

```
operator fun get(key: K): V? {
    val index = indexOfKey(key)
    return if (index >= 0) array[(index shl 1) + 1] as V? else null
}
```

It basically tries to get the index of the given `key`, and if it is a positive value, then it returns the value present at the index position of `(index * 2) + 1` in the data array. Let's see how it gets the index of the given `key`:

```
fun indexOfKey(key: K): Int {
    return if (key == null) indexOfNull() else indexOf(key)
}
```

If you remember the `put` operation explanation, these two methods were used there too. As both of these methods' logic are similar, we'll look at the details of one method only. The following code is the implementation of the `indexOf()` method:

```
private fun indexOf(key: K): Int {
    val hash = key!!.hashCode()

    if (size == 0) return 0.inv()
    val index = Arrays.binarySearch(hashes, 0, size, hash)

    // Key not found, return -ve value
    if (index < 0) return index

    if (key == array[index shl 1]) return index

    // Search for a matching key after the index.
    var end = index + 1
    while (end < size && hashes[end] == hash) {
        if (key == array[end shl 1]) return end
        end++
    }

    // Search for a matching key before the index.
    var i = index - 1
    while (i >= 0 && hashes[i] == hash) {
        if (key == array[i shl 1]) return i
        i--
    }
    return end.inv()
}
```

Let's understand the preceding method's logic step by step:

1. First, we get the hash value of `key`. In the case of `indexOfNull()`, it is 0.
2. Check whether `ArrayMap` is empty or not. If it is empty, then return –1.
3. Check whether the hash value calculated in *step 1* is present in the hash array or not. If it isn't present, then return the value resulted by the search.

4. If the `hash` is found in the hash array, check whether the `key` in the respective index is equal to the input `key`. If it's the same, return the index as the result. In case of `indexOfNull()`, we need to check for `null`, as the `key` here is `null`.

 The comparison of keys is necessary because there might be the possibility of a hash collision.

5. If `key` doesn't match in *step 4*, then traverse linearly in both directions through the data array and compare the keys with the input `key` until it is found.

6. If we still don't get the required `key`, then it is certain that the input `key` had the same `hash` as a different existing `key`. So, return the inverse of the index at which we stopped our search.

 Returning the inverse of the index is necessary for two reasons. First, as it is a negative value, it indicates that the required `key` is not present. Second, if the `key` is for a `put` operation, the negative index gives the value for the place where the new entry should go. For more information, check the previous section, putting a key-value pair into `ArrayMap`, where we discussed the `put` operation. Note that we have done an `inv()` call on the result of this method.

Removing a key-value pair from ArrayMap

Here is the code for this operation:

```
fun remove(key: K): V? {
    val index = indexOfKey(key)
    if (index >= 0) return removeAt(index)
    return null
}
```

It simply checks the index of a given `key`, and if it is a positive value, it calls `removeAt()` with the resulting index; otherwise, it returns `null`. Now, let's see how `removeAt()` is implemented:

```
private fun removeAt(index: Int): V? {
    val oldVal = array[(index shl 1) + 1]
    val newSize = size - 1
    if (size <= 1) {
        // Empty Map
        hashes = IntArray(0)
        array = arrayOf()
    } else {
        System.arraycopy(hashes, index + 1, hashes, index, newSize - index)
        System.arraycopy(array, (index + 1) shl 1, array, index shl 1,
(newSize - index) shl 1)
        array[newSize shl 1] = null
        array[(newSize shl 1) + 1] = null
    }
    size = newSize
    return oldVal as V
}
```

Here is a step-by-step guide to how it works:

1. Before removing the key-value pair, it gets the existing value to return to the caller.
2. Then, it checks the size of `ArrayMap`. If it is 1 or less, then it is probably either empty or has only one entry. So, we make both the arrays empty.
3. If `ArrayMap` is not empty, then it shifts the index of the hash array by 1 and the data array backward by 2. For example, if index 4 needs to be removed, then all the `hashes` from index 5 onward will move by 1 index position backward (hash 5 will be at 4, hash 6 will be at 5, and so on). The same thing applies to the data array.
4. Now the last two indexes of data array have garbage data, so assign them with `null`.
5. Decrement the size of `ArrayMap` by 1 and return the old value.

Summary

So far, we have learned two different implementation of Map (`HashMap` and `ArrayMap`). Now, *when to use what* is an obvious question. To answer that, we have to remember how they work. As we know, `HashMap` requires more memory than `ArrayMap`, so we choose `HashMap` if memory is a constraint for us. Is memory the only parameter you should consider? Of course not. You are using these data structures to do some operations on them. We know that for the `put` operation in `ArrayMap`, we need to allocate new arrays and do the array copy operation, so it is a heavier operation in `ArrayMap` than in `HashMap`. The same thing applies with the `remove` operation, but the `get (fetch)` operation in `ArrayMap` is faster than `HashMap` as it uses binary search. So, we can conclude that if more operation is `get (non mutable)`, then use `ArrayMap`; otherwise use `HashMap`.

Work	HashMap	ArrayMap
Memory	More required	Less required
Fetch operation	Slower	Faster
Insert operation	Faster	Slower
Delete operation	Faster	Slower

 Faster and *slower* are used only in the context of these two data structures. The same thing applies with less or more memory.

Questions.

1. Modify HashMap to have a constructor which accepts a Map<K, V> object to create itself.
2. Implement a Map whose keys are primitive integers.

Section 3: Algorithms and Efficiency 3

Just learning about various data structures is insufficient if your desire is to master computer programming; you also need to learn about algorithms. This section will walk you through the popular searching and sorting algorithms, along with their implementation with Kotlin. You'll also learn about the efficiencies of these algorithms, so that you can wisely decide which algorithm to implement when you're writing a program.

The following chapters will be covered in this section:

- Chapter 6, *Deep-Dive into Searching Algorithms*
- Chapter 7, *Understanding Sorting Algorithms*

6
Deep-Dive into Searching Algorithms

Searching is one of the trivial operations that we usually perform when dealing with a collection. We can define it as finding an item from among a group of items (or a collection). As technology evolves, we accumulate more and more data. To then find specific information in these huge datasets, we need to have some kind of algorithm that will do the job for us quickly.

Searching can be done in many ways. In this chapter, we'll discuss a few of the most commonly used search algorithms:

- Linear search
- Binary search
- Jump search
- Exponential search
- Pattern search

Technical requirements

There are no specific requirements here. To practice the algorithms and data structures we'll learn from this book, we need the Kotlin compiler to be installed on our PC.

The GitHub repository for the book is located here:

```
https://github.com/PacktPublishing/Hands-On-Data-Structures-and-Algorithms-
with-Kotlin/tree/master/Chapter06
```

Understanding the searching algorithm

To understand searching better, consider the following example.

Let's say that you've 500 students in your school. One day, your principal asks you to locate one student, but you've only been given some details about them. You can do this task in multiple ways. Let's explore a couple of possible approaches:

- **Approach 1**: You can go and visit each of the students and check if they are the student your principal has asked for. This will take quite a long time, as your search might end with the very last student.
- **Approach 2**: Instead of visiting each student randomly, you can check which class the student belongs to, and only visit the students from that class. This will significantly reduce your search time.

From the preceding two approaches, it's obvious that you'll always choose the second one because it significantly reduces your time and effort to complete the task. And using searching algorithms is equivalent to using the second approach.

Searching algorithms allow us to quickly find an item or items from a collection. However, their performance is dependent on the way the items are stored in the collection. For example, the second approach mentioned above is faster because the school had stored information about the students in an organized manner.

As mentioned earlier, we'll be looking at five types of searching algorithm. Let's begin with linear search.

Linear search

When we try to find an element in a collection by checking each element of the collection one by one, we refer to this way of searching as a **linear search**. We can perform a linear search for both unordered and ordered collections.

Linear search in an unordered collection

As the elements in an unordered collection are not in a clear and logical order, we've to check each element until we find the required one. The code for such a linear search will look like the following:

```
fun <E> Collection<E>.linearSearch(element: E): Int {
    for ((index, value) in this.withIndex()) {
```

```
        if (value == element) return index
    }
    return -1
}
```

One thing to note here is that the function is defined as an extension to the `Collection` interface, so we can call `linearSearch()` directly on the collection object as if were part of `Collection` interface. The following is an example:

```
val languages = arrayListOf("Python", "Java", "Kotlin", "Scala")
println("Kotlin is at - ${languages.linearSearch("Kotlin")}")
```

Linear search in an ordered collection

If the elements in a collection are in the proper order, linear search performs well if the searched element is not present in the collection. The following is the code:

```
fun <E : Comparable<E>> Collection<E>.searchInSortedCollection(element: E):
Int {
    for ((index, value) in this.withIndex()) {
        if (value == element) return index
        else if (value > element) return -1
    }
    return -1
}
```

If you observe closely, you can see that, in addition to checking whether the value is equal to the required element, we also check if the iterated value is greater than the required element in order to decide whether further elements in the collection could be possible matches.

Here, in addition to the equality check, we also checked which is greater, so type E should implement a `Comparable` interface.

Binary search

Binary search is one of the most widely used search algorithms and gives the best performance in worst-case scenarios. As discussed in the previous section, linear search can perform at $O(n)$ in the worst case, whereas binary search uses divide-and-conquer techniques to perform the search as fast as $O(log\ n)$.

Though *binary search* is faster in performance, it can only be applied if the collection is already sorted. If the collection is not sorted, then *linear search* is the only way to perform the search.

Working with binary search

Let's say you've an ArrayList of size n and you're trying to find the index of x. To perform a binary search over the ArrayList to find x, you need to follow these steps:

1. Go to the middle element and compare it with x
2. If the middle element is greater, then the left half has x
3. If the middle element is smaller, then the right half has x
4. Now that we know which half has x, consider that half as the input array, and repeat from *step 1* for that half

Refer to this diagram as an example of an array containing numbers. Using the steps listed above, we are attempting the find the number 142 in the array:

| 6 | 17 | 23 | 38 | 42 | 67 | (71) | 95 | 102 | 137 | 142 | 159 | 203 | Let's search 142 / Go to the mid element |

| 6 | 17 | 23 | 38 | 42 | 67 | 71 | 95 | 102 | (137) | 142 | 159 | 203 | 142 > 71 / Search further at right half / Go to the mid of right half |

| 6 | 17 | 23 | 38 | 42 | 67 | 71 | 95 | 102 | 137 | 142 | (159) | 203 | 142 > 137 / Search further at right half / Go to the mid of right half |

| 6 | 17 | 23 | 38 | 42 | 67 | 71 | 95 | 102 | 137 | (142) | 159 | 203 | 142 < 159 / Search further at left half / Go to the mid of left half |

| 6 | 17 | 23 | 38 | 42 | 67 | 71 | 95 | 102 | 137 | 142 | 159 | 203 | 142 = 142 / Element found / Return the index |

Check the following snippet to understand how the preceding steps work in the code:

```
fun <E: Comparable<E>> List<E>.binarySearch(element: E): Int {
    var left = 0
    var right = size - 1
    while (left <= right) {
        var mid = (left + right) / 2
        val midVal = this[mid]
        val compare = midVal.compareTo(element)

        if (compare < 0) left = mid + 1
        else if (compare > 0) right = mid - 1
        else return mid // element found
    }
    return -1 // element not found
}
```

As we are skipping half of the elements in every iteration, it's considered to be one of the fastest search algorithms.

Jump search

Jump search is a slightly modified version of linear search. Instead of searching each index, we jump a few indexes by a fixed number of steps. There is no rule on how many steps we should skip in every iteration.

Let's consider an example to understand this better. Imagine that we've a large array of [1, 5, 7, 12, 18, 25, 37, 49, 62, 73, 89, 103, ...] and we want to search for a number (62 here). We'll perform the following steps:

1. Check if the value at index 0 (1 here) is equal to x (62 here).
2. If yes, the search is complete.
3. If no, jump to index 5 (25 here) and check whether the value is equal to x (62). We skipped 5 indexes here.
4. There might be many cases where the number might not be present in the array or list. In those cases, we need to stop the search operation as soon as possible. So repeat step 3 until we find a number equal to or greater than x. Now we are at index 10 (89 here), which is greater than x (62 here).
5. We are sure that the number x is in between indexes 5 and 10. So, do a linear search here until we find x (62).

Choosing indexes to be skipped

In the preceding example, we chose to skip five indexes, but we can find the optimal number to be skipped so that our algorithm performance is also optimal. To find this optimal number, we need to consider the worst-case scenario.

Suppose we've an array of size n and we want to skip m indexes at every iteration. In the worst case, we'll perform n/m jumps and $m-1$ iterations for linear search. So, our final performance will be $f(n) = (n/m) + (m - 1) = n + m^2 - m$, and the optimal value of m could be $\sqrt{n}$.

The code looks like this:

```
fun <E: Comparable<E>> Array<E>.jumpSearch(element: E): Int {
    val size = this.size
    var step = Math.sqrt(size.toDouble()).toInt()
    var prev = 0

    while (this[Math.min(step, size) - 1] < element) {
        prev = step
        step *= 2
        if (prev >= size.toInt()) return -1
    }

    while(this[prev] < element) {
        prev++
        if (prev == Math.min(step, size)) return -1
    }

    if (this[prev] == element) {
        return prev
    }
    return -1
}
```

The preceding snippet has three parts to it:

- **Part 1**: The first `while` loop jumps to the indexes until it finds a value greater than the search element.
- **Part 2**: Next, the `while` loop does a linear search from the `prev` index until it finds a value greater than the search element, or reaches the last index.
- **Part 3**: This just checks whether the previous `while` loop is terminated because the search element was found. If so, it returns the `prev` index as the result index, or returns -1, meaning not found.

Exponential search

Like jump search, this is also a modified version of the linear search algorithm. It works as follows:

1. **Step 1**: We jump to indexes exponentially. Here, the jump step would be 1, 2, 4, 8, 16,...,i/2, i, 2i, 4i,... Notice that this is the same as *jump search*.
2. **Step 2**: We keep on jumping the steps exponentially until we get a value greater than the search element. Notice that this is also the same as we did in *jump search*.
3. **Step 3**: Once we get a value greater than the search element (for example, at the *i* index), we are sure that the search element is between the $i/2^{th}$ and i^{th} index. Notice that this is also the same as *jump search*.
4. **Step 4**: Now do a *binary search* between these two indexes.

As all the steps followed here are similar to the jump search technique (except the last one, where we do a binary search instead), use any of the existing examples and perform this search on your own as a learning exercise.

Pattern search

So far, we've checked how to search for an element in an array or list. A *string* is also an array of characters, and we can apply different search algorithms to search for a character in a string. For example, searching for character t from the Kotlin string can be done using any of the aforementioned algorithms.

But what if we want to search for a pattern in a given string? For example, imagine that we need to search for the substring of in the string Kotlin is one of the best languages in the modern programming language world. In this case, both the input value and the pattern to be searched are strings themselves, so, the aforementioned algorithms will not work.

In this section, we'll understand how to search for a pattern in a string. Though it can be done in many ways, we'll discuss the four most-used pattern-search algorithms:

- Naive pattern search
- The Rabin-Karp algorithm
- Finite Automaton
- The Knuth-Morris-Pratt algorithm

Naive pattern search

This is a brute-force technique with which to search for a pattern in a text string. In this case, we need to search for the pattern from the beginning of the text until we find it. If m is the pattern length and n is the text length, then the complexity here becomes $O(m * n)$.

How Naive pattern search works

Let's say we want to search for the OT pattern in the text string HELLO KOTLIN!!!. We'll need to perform the following steps to find it:

1. Get the length of the pattern m and the text n.
2. Iterate over the text from the 0th to the $(n-m)^{th}$ index.
3. For each iteration, do a comparison with the pattern. This is done using another iteration over the pattern from the 0th to the mth index.
4. If the inner iteration is completed successfully, that means the pattern is found. Otherwise, repeat steps 2 and 3 until we have scanned the full text.

The code looks like this:

```
fun search(text: String, pattern: String): Int {
    var retVal = -1
    val patternLen = pattern.length
    val len = text.length - patternLen
    for (i in 0 until len) {
        var isFound = true
        for (j in 0 until patternLen) {
            if (text[i + j] != pattern[j]) {
                isFound = false
                break
            }
        }
        if (isFound) {
            retVal = i
            break
        }
    }
    return retVal
}
```

If you observe closely, you can see that we've declared a Boolean flag to identify whether the inner loop has successfully completed all the iterations, or was broken in between. If the inner `for` loop is looped until the end, that means the pattern is found.

The Rabin-Karp algorithm

This is another substring search algorithm that uses hashing to do its job. As we've already read in detail about hashing and its benefits in Chapter 5, *Maps – Working with Key-value Pairs*, we'll not discuss it again. Instead, we'll create a hash function here and use that to do the search operation.

The basic idea of this algorithm is to compare the hash value of the pattern with the hash value of each substring of text (which is the same length as the pattern), and if they are found to be equal, then we go ahead with the string comparison. Here are the steps we need to follow:

1. Calculate the hash value of the pattern
2. Get the length of both the pattern *m* and the text *n*
3. Iterate over the text from the 0th to the $(n-m)^{th}$ index
4. For each iteration, calculate the hash value of a substring of size *m* and then compare it with the hash value of the pattern, calculated in step 1
5. If both hash values are found to be equal, then compare the corresponding substring with the pattern
6. Repeat steps 4 and 5 until the pattern is matched or the text has been scanned fully

Hash functions for Rabin-Karp

There is no defined rule for generating a hash value only in one particular way. You can definitely choose your own method as per your needs. We chose the following method for this book:

```
private fun hash(input: String): Long {
    var result = 0L
    input.forEachIndexed { index, char ->
        result += (char.toDouble() * Math.pow(97.0,
index.toDouble()))).toLong()
    }
    return result
}
```

To understand more about the way the hash is generated, let's check the following diagram:

From the preceding image, it's quite clear that we've used the formula $ASCII * 97^{index}$ to calculate the hash value. So, the hash value of KOTLIN would be $75 * 97^0 + 79 * 97^1 + 84 * 97^2 + 76 * 97^3 + 73 * 97^4 + 78 * 97^5$.

A few important points to note here:

1. **97** is a prime number; you can use any number of your choice. Choosing a slightly higher prime number generates a good hash value
2. We've chosen to generate hash values in Long instead of Int to avoid the integer cycle problem for a larger pattern
3. While calculating the hash, we've cast everything into Double just to make it work with the Math.pow() API

Rolled-hash functions for Rabin-Karp

Let's say we've the following text, Out of all modern JVM languages Kotlin is the best and I love Kotlin so much, and we need to search for Kotlin in it.

As we know that the pattern here is of length 6, we need to calculate the hash value for substrings from the following indexes of $0^{th}..5^{th}$, $1^{st}..6^{th}$, $2^{nd}..7^{th}$, and so on. Note carefully that in the 2nd iteration, while calculating the hash value of the $1^{st}..6^{th}$ indexed substring, we can reuse the hash value of the 1st iteration. This makes us avoid recalculating the hash value of many characters repeatedly.

For example, to calculate the hash value of the $1^{st}..6^{th}$ indexed substring, we can use the hash value of the $0^{th}..5^{th}$ indexed substring calculated in the previous iteration:

- Subtract the hash value for the 0th character and add the hash value for the 6th character

This is done using the `rolledHash` function. The following is the code to do so:

```
private fun rolledHash(oldChar: Char, newChar: Char,
    oldHash: Long, patternLen: Int): Long {
    val newHash = (((oldHash - oldChar.toLong()) / 97) +
        newChar.toDouble() * Math.pow(97.0, (patternLen -
1).toDouble()))).toLong()
    return newHash
}
```

Searching using hash values

We now understand how the hash values are calculated, so now we just need to use them to search the pattern. The following is the code for that:

```
fun search(text: String, pattern: String): Int {
    val patternLen = pattern.length
    val textLen = text.length - patternLen
    val patternHash = hash(pattern)
    var subText = text.substring(0, patternLen)
    var subTextHash = hash(subText)
    var isFound = false
    if ((patternHash == subTextHash)
            and subText.equals(pattern))
        return 0

    for (i in 1..textLen) {
        subTextHash = rolledHash(text[i - 1], text[i + patternLen - 1],
subTextHash, patternLen)
        if ((patternHash == subTextHash)
            and text.substring(i, i + patternLen).equals(pattern))
    return i
    }
    return -1
}
```

Note that we are using the `hash` function to calculate the hash value for the 1st time, and from the 2nd time onwards we use the `rolledHash` function.

Performance

The Rabin-Karp algorithm performs better than the naive way of pattern searching. Its complexity varies from $O(m + n)$ in the best case, to $O(m * n)$ in the worst-case.

The Knuth-Morris-Pratt algorithm

The **Knuth-Morris-Pratt** (**KMP**) search algorithm is one of the most efficient algorithms used for pattern searching. In both the previously discussed methods of pattern searching, we've to traverse each character of the text multiple times.

KMP search shines in this regard by finding a way to not traverse the same index of the text again after it has been traversed once. This is achieved by precomputing the pattern to form an array with prefixed values.

The prefix function

To understand this function better, consider the following example.

Let's say we are searching for a b a b a a in the text a b a b d a b d b c d a b d c b d a b a b a a c b d b c d a b c d b c d a a a b a b a a c c d d c b c a. The search starts from the 0th index, and the mismatch happens at the 4th index.

As the basic idea behind KMP search is not to traverse backward, we've got to find a way to start the next search from the 4th index, instead of the 1st index. To do this, let's analyze the substring of the pattern prior to the 4th index, which is a b a b.

Now we've got to check whether there are any prefixes that are also suffixes. And in this case, a b is a prefix as well as a suffix. This makes it clear that in the text, before the 4th index, a b is present. So, instead of starting the search from the 1st index, we can skip two indexes from the pattern and start comparing the 4th index of the text to the 3rd index of the pattern. The following is the way it looks in the next iteration:

a b a b d a b d b c d a b d c b d a b a b a a c b d b c d a b c d b c d a a a b a b a a c c d d c b c a a b a b a a

Here, the search started from the 4th index and the mismatch happened at the 4th index.

Please note that even though we shifted the pattern to two indexes, our comparison started from the 3rd index of the pattern and the 4th index of the text, which means we didn't move backward.

Now that we've understood how to skip a few indexes based on the prefix-suffix information of the pattern, this prefix information can be calculated by a function and stored in an array. The following is the code which shows this in operation:

```
fun preparePrefixArray(pattern: String): IntArray {
    val patternLen = pattern.length
    val arr = IntArray(patternLen)
    var index = 0
    var i = 1
    while(i < patternLen) {
        if (pattern[i] == pattern[index]) {
            arr[i] = index + 1
            index++
            i++
        } else {
            if (index != 0) index = arr[index - 1]
            else {
                arr[i] = 0
                i++
            }
        }
    }
    return arr
}
```

Searching using a prefix array

Now let's use this precomputed prefix array to do our search:

```
fun search(text: String, pattern: String): Int {
    val prefixArr = preparePrefixArray(pattern)
    val textLen = text.length
    val patternLen = pattern.length

    var patternIndex = 0
    var textIndex = 0
    while ((textIndex < textLen) and (patternIndex < patternLen)) {
      if (pattern[patternIndex] == text[textIndex]) {
          textIndex++
          patternIndex++
      } else {
        // Use the prefix array to skip few indexes
```

```
        if (patternIndex != 0) patternIndex = prefixArr[patternIndex - 1]
        else textIndex++
    }
    if (patternIndex == patternLen) {
        // We found the pattern
        return textIndex - patternIndex
    }
}
return -1
}
```

A few important steps to note from the above algorithm are as follows:

1. Prepare the prefix array from the given pattern.
2. Start comparing the characters from the 0th index of both the pattern and text.
3. Iterate until we reach the end of both the text and pattern.
4. If the characters at `patternIndex` and `textIndex` are the same, then increment them by 1.
5. If they are not the same, then a mismatch has happened. So use the prefix array calculated at step-1 to skip a few indexes.
6. Continue step 4 and step 5 until `patternIndex` is not equal to `patternLen` or we reach at the end of both the text and pattern.

Summary

In this chapter, we learned about a few of the most commonly used search algorithms. See the following table for a comparison of their relative performances. This will give you a better understanding when you come to choose which algorithm to use yourself:

Algorithm	Performance
Linear Search	$O(n)$
Binary Search	$O(\log n)$
Jump Search	$O(\sqrt{n})$
Exponential Search	$O(\log n)$

Here, n is the size of the collection.

In addition to item search algorithms, we've also covered a few commonly used pattern matching algorithms. Here is a comparison of their relative performance:

Algorithm	Performance
Naive Pattern Search	$O(m * n)$
Rabin-Karp Search	$O(m * n)$
Knuth-Morris-Prath Search	$O(m) + O(k) = O(n + k)$

Here, m is the length of the text, n is the length of the pattern and k is the length of temporary array created for KMP search (the same as the pattern length).

There are tons of examples that use efficient search algorithms to run their business. Search engines serach as Google and Bing are the best examples we can think of. In addition to these, we can also think of any database query which sends us the result so fast by applying some advanced search techniques.

We have already understood that search algorithms work best if the items are sorted. So the `Chapter 7`, *Understanding Sorting Algorithms*, will help us to know how sorting algorithms work and how they help.

Questions

1. Write an algorithm to find k[th] largest element of an integer array.
2. Write a snippet which tells whether a given array or list has a duplicate element or not.
3. Find all the occurrences of a pattern from a text using any pattern matching algorithm discussed in the chapter.

7
Understanding Sorting Algorithms

Whenever we are dealing with a collection of data (whether a list or an array), we might need algorithms to sort the data in order to make other operations faster. For example, searching an element from a list or merging two lists into one work best when the lists are sorted. If the data is sorted, it also makes tasks such as generating human-readable reports easy.

There are many algorithms for sorting a list or an array. In this chapter, we'll try to explain a few of the most commonly used sorting algorithms and how they work internally. The algorithms we are going to discuss here are as follows:

- Bubble sort
- Selection sort
- Insertion sort
- Merge sort
- Quick sort
- Heap sort

Technical requirements

There are no specific requirements here. To practice the algorithms and data structures that we'll learn in this book, we need the Kotlin compiler to be installed on our PC.

The GitHub repository containing the code for this chapter can be found at this URL: `https://github.com/PacktPublishing/Hands-On-Data-Structures-and-Algorithms-with-Kotlin/tree/master/Chapter07`.

Understanding the bubble sort algorithm

This is the simplest sorting algorithm. In this algorithm, we just go through each item in the collection, compare two adjacent items, and swap them if they are not in the required order. We do this repetitively until no swaps are required.

You can consider this as one of the brute force techniques for sorting a collection. The complexity of this algorithm is $O(n^2)$ and it is considered one of the slowest sorting algorithms. The only reason we can use this algorithm is its simple implementation.

How the bubble sort algorithm works

Bubble sort simply traverses the collection and compares the adjacent elements to check whether they are in the right order or not. If they are in the proper order, then it compares the next two adjacent elements; otherwise, it swaps those two elements before moving on to the next comparison.

By doing this, it makes sure that at the end of every iteration, one element will be sorted. All the examples we cover further in this chapter will be for sorting a collection in ascending order. For descending order, the comparison changes from < to >, but the algorithm remains the same. The following diagram should make this clearer:

Note that the preceding diagram doesn't have all the iterations, as it was difficult to fit everything into the diagram, so it's unsorted. The following description has all the iterations to support the preceding diagram.

Let's consider the preceding example and understand bubble sort step by step:

Iteration 1:

17 12 29 21 5 7	Our input, compares if 17 < 12, and swaps.
12 17 29 21 5 7	This compares if 17 < 29, in order, so ignores.
12 17 29 21 5 7	This compares if 29 < 21, and swaps.
12 17 21 29 5 7	This compares if 29 < 5, and swaps.
12 17 21 5 29 7	This compares if 29 < 7, and swaps.
12 17 21 5 7 **29**	Iteration 1 is completed and **29** is sorted now.

Iteration 2:

12 17 21 5 7 **29**	This compares if 12 < 17, in order, so ignores.
12 17 21 5 7 **29**	This compares if 17 < 21, in order, so ignores.
12 17 21 5 7 **29**	This compares if 21 < 5, and swaps.
12 17 5 21 7 **29**	This compares if 21 < 7, and swaps.
12 17 5 7 **21 29**	Iteration 2 is completed and **21 29** are sorted.

Iteration 3:

12 17 5 7 **21 29**	This compares if 12 < 17, in order, so ignores.
12 17 5 7 **21 29**	This compares if 17 < 5, and swaps.
12 5 17 7 **21 29**	This compares if 17 < 7, and swaps.
12 5 7 **17 21 29**	Iteration 3 is completed and **17 21 29** are sorted.

Iteration 4:

12 5 7 **17 21 29**	This compares if 12 < 5, and swaps.
5 12 7 **17 21 29**	This compares if 12 < 7, and swaps.
5 7 **12 17 21 29**	Iteration 4 is completed and **12 17 21 29** are sorted.

Iteration 5:

5 7 **12 17 21 29**	This compares if 5 < 7, in order, so ignores.
5 7 12 17 21 29	There are no further elements for comparison. This means the whole collection is sorted.

Implementing bubble sort

So , we have understood the concept of bubble sort. The following snippet is the final implementation of the aforementioned theory:

```kotlin
fun <E: Comparable<E>> MutableList<E>.sort() {
    val len = size
    for (i in 0 until (len - 1)) {
        for (j in 0 until (len - i - 1)) {
            if (this[j].compareTo(this[j + 1]) > 0) {
                val temp = this[j]
                this[j] = this[j + 1]
                this[j + 1] = temp
            }
        }
    }
}
```

The preceding snippet is an extension function for `MutableList`. But we can do it for Array, as well as List also. For an immutable list, we need to create a separate list and insert the elements in a sorted order to return the final sorted list.

Understanding selection sort

Selection sort performs with the same complexity to bubble sort. Its complexity is also $O(n^2)$.

How the selection sort algorithm works

This works exactly the opposite as bubble sort, in terms of ordering the elements. Bubble sort sorts one element at every iteration and freezes its index toward the end of the collection. In contrast to that, selection sort sorts one element at every iteration and freezes its index toward the start of the collection.

You can imagine it as two subarrays, one sorted and another unsorted. In the beginning, the sorted subarray is empty and the unsorted subarray is the whole array given as input. To do this, it finds the smallest element (or the largest, if sorting in descending order) from the unsorted subarray and puts it toward the beginning of the array (or the end of the sorted subarray).

To understand more, let's consider the same example we discussed previously, and sort it using this algorithm:

Iteration 1:

17 12 29 21 5 7	Our input, results in 12 as the minimum between 17 and 12
17 12 29 21 5 7	This results in 12 as the minimum between 12 and 29
17 12 29 21 5 7	This results in 12 as the minimum between 12 and 21
17 12 29 21 5 7	This results in 5 as the minimum between 12 and 5
17 12 29 21 5 7	This results in 5 as the minimum between 5 and 7
5 12 29 21 17 7	This swaps in 17 and 5 and freezes the 0th index

Iteration 2:

5 12 29 21 17 7	This results in 12 as the minimum between 12 and 29
5 12 29 21 17 7	This results in 12 as the minimum between 12 and 21
5 12 29 21 17 7	This results in 12 as the minimum between 12 and 17
5 12 29 21 17 7	This results in 7 as the minimum between 12 and 7
5 7 29 21 17 12	This swaps 7 and 12 and freezes the 1st index

Iteration 3:

5 7 29 21 17 12	This results in 21 as the minimum between 29 and 21
5 7 29 21 17 12	This results in 17 as the minimum between 21 and 17
5 7 29 21 17 12	This results in 12 as the minimum between 17 and 12
5 7 12 21 17 29	This swaps 12 and 29 and freezes the 2nd index

Iteration 4:

5 7 12 21 17 29	This results in 17 as the minimum between 21 and 17
5 7 12 21 17 29	This results in 17 as the minimum between 17 and 29
5 7 12 17 21 29	This swaps 17 and 21 and freezes the 3rd index

Iteration 5:

5 7 12 17 21 29	This results in 21 as the minimum between 21 and 29
5 7 12 17 21 29	No swapping is required and as no further elements are left, we can conclude that the collection is fully sorted

Implementing selection sort

The following code snippet is the final implementation of the aforementioned theory:

```
fun <E: Comparable<E>> MutableList<E>.sort() {
    val len = size
    // Find the minimum value of the array
    for (i in 0 until (len - 1)) {
        // Getting the index where minimum value is present
        var minIndex = i
        for (j in (i + 1) until len) {
            if (this[j].compareTo(this[minIndex]) < 0) minIndex = j
        }

        // We got the minimum element, now swap that to first element
        val temp = this[minIndex]
        this[minIndex] = this[i]
        this[i] = temp
    }
}
```

Understanding insertion sort

Insertion sort performs slightly better than the previously discussed algorithms. Its complexity is $O(n^2)$. Though it has the same complexity as bubble sort and selection sort, it sorts faster than both of these in most cases. One of the best use cases for using this algorithm is to sort a dynamic collection. If you have a dynamic collection where items will keep on getting added to it at runtime, it can be sorted very efficiently by using insertion sort as and when the item reaches.

How the insertion sort algorithm works

The insertion sort algorithm has two subarrays (one sorted and another unsorted). Initially, the sorted subarray has only one item (the item at the 0th index) and the unsorted subarray has items from the 1st to nth indexes. In every iteration, it takes one item from the start of the unsorted subarray and puts it in its proper place in the sorted subarray. At the end, the sorted subarray becomes an array of size n and the unsorted subarray becomes empty. Now, we understand that picking an item from the unsorted subarray is done from the start, but how does it find the proper place to put it in the sorted subarray? The answer this is that it does a linear search in the sorted subarray to find the right index for the item it picked from the unsorted subarray.

Let's use the same example we used already, and sort it using insertion sort:

Iteration 1:

17 12 29 21 5 7	Our input, checks 12 < 17 and puts 17 at the 1st index.
12 17 29 21 5 7	Puts 12 at 0th index; now 12 and 17 are sorted.

Iteration 2:

12 17 29 21 5 7	Checks 29 < 17 and skips.
12 17 29 21 5 7	Now 12, 17 and 29 are sorted.

Iteration 3:

12 17 29 21 5 7	Checks 21 < 29 and puts 29 at the 3rd index
12 17 X 29 5 7	Checks 21 < 17 and skips

At this point in time, the 3rd index has a garbage value, and the picked value `21` is stored in the `temp` variable.

12 17 21 29 5 7	21 is stored at the 3rd index from the `temp` variable. Now 12, 17, 21 and 29 are sorted.

Iteration 4:

12 17 21 29 5 7	Checks 5 < 29 and puts 29 at the 4th index.
12 17 21 X 29 7	Checks 5 < 21 and puts 21 at the 3rd index.
12 17 X 21 29 7	Checks 5 < 17 and puts 17 at the 2nd index.
12 X 17 21 29 7	Checks 5 < 12 and puts 12 at the 1st index.
X 12 17 21 29 7	Checks 5 < 12 and puts 12 at the 1st index.
5 12 17 21 29 7	5 from `temp` variable is put at the 0th index. Now 5, 12, 17, 21 and 29 are sorted.

Iteration 5:

5 12 17 21 29 7	Checks 7 < 29 and puts 29 at the 5th index.
5 12 17 21 X 29	Checks 7 < 21 and puts 21 at the 4th index.
5 12 17 X 21 29	Checks 7 < 17 and puts 17 at the 3rd index.
5 12 X 17 21 29	Checks 7 < 12 and puts 12 at the 2nd index.
5 X 12 17 21 29	Checks 7 < 5 and skips.
5 7 12 17 21 29	Puts 7 at the 1st index from `temp` variable.

Now, all are sorted.

Implementing insertion sort

The following code snippet is the final implementation of the aforementioned concept:

```
fun <E: Comparable<E>> MutableList<E>.sort() {
    val len = size
    for (i in 1 until len) {
        var key = this[i]
        var j = i - 1;

        while(j >= 0 && this[j].compareTo(key) > 0) {
            this[j + 1] = this[j]
            j--
        }
        this[j + 1] = key
    }
}
```

 To put an item at its proper index inside the sorted subarray, we used linear search in the previous example. We can also use binary search for this purpose, which would make this algorithm even faster.

Understanding merge sort

Merge sort is one of the fastest sorting algorithms, and is used widely by many programmers. It sorts the elements using a divide and conquer algorithm. This makes it even faster for sorting huge datasets with the help of multiple machines simultaneously. The complexity of merge sort is $O(n \log n)$, which is considered to be the shortest possible time required for sorting n number of elements.

How the merge sort algorithm works

As we already know that it works using he divide and conquer principle, let's understand how it really divides the input to do the job. It sorts any input list as follows:

1. It divides the input list (unsorted) into two sublists from the middle index. Now the algorithm has two sublists as input.
2. It repeats *step 1* until each sublist has only one element (that is, *size = 1*).

3. Now, it starts merging each sublist until all sublists are merged. While merging, it sorts the elements of those two sublists.

Let's consider the preceding example and see how merge sort works:

Iteration 1:

17 12 29 21 5 7	Our input, gets divided into two parts, 17 12 29 and 21 5 7

Iteration 2:

17 12 29	Our input, gets divided into two parts, 17 12 and 29

Iteration 3:

17 12	Our input, gets divided into two parts, 17 and 12

Iteration 4:

17 and 12	Our input get merged as 12 17
12 17 and 29	Our input get merged as 12 17 29

Iteration 5:

21 5 7	Our input, gets divided into two parts, 21 5 and 7

Iteration 6:

21 5	Our input, gets divided into two parts, 21 and 5

Iteration 7:

21 and 5	Our input get merged as 5 21
5 21 and 7	Our input get merged as 5 7 21

Iteration 8:

12 17 29 and 5 7 21	Our input get merged as 5 7 12 17 21 29

 The `Iteration <n>` mentioned previously is not how iterations are represented in real code. It's used to help you understand better.

Implementing merge sort

As we have seen, merge sort consists of two major jobs—dividing and merging—so we have created two separate functions accordingly, as follows:

```
fun <E: Comparable<E>> Array<E>.sort(): Array<E> {
    if (size <= 1) return this

    val middle = size / 2
    val left = copyOfRange(0, middle)
    val right = copyOfRange(middle, size)
    return merge(this, left.sort(), right.sort())
}
```

The preceding snippet is the `sort` API exposed to the outside world. The following is a step-by-step description of the preceding code snippet:

1. If the array size is `1`, then it's already sorted, so return the same array
2. Otherwise, get the middle index
3. Create two sublists, left (`0..middle`) and right (`middle..size`)
4. Now, it recursively calls the sort API to create further smaller sublists
5. Finally, it calls the `merge` function (a private API) with the sublists created in *step 3* and *step 4*

Here is what the `merge` function looks like:

```
private fun <E: Comparable<E>> merge(arr: Array<E>, left: Array<E>, right:
Array<E>): Array<E> {
    val leftArrSize = left.size
    val rightArrSize = right.size
    var leftArrIndex = 0
    var rightArrIndex = 0
    var index = 0
    while(leftArrIndex < leftArrSize && rightArrIndex < rightArrSize) {
        if (left[leftArrIndex] <= right[rightArrIndex]) {
            arr[index] = left[leftArrIndex]
            leftArrIndex++
        } else {
            arr[index] = right[rightArrIndex]
            rightArrIndex++
        }
        index++
    }

    while(leftArrIndex < leftArrSize) {
        arr[index] = left[leftArrIndex]
```

```
            leftArrIndex++
            index++
    }

    while(rightArrIndex < rightArrSize) {
        arr[index] = right[rightArrIndex]
        rightArrIndex++
        index++
    }
    return arr
}
```

Here is a step-by-step description of the preceding `merge` function:

1. It takes a few pieces of metadata, such as left subarray size, right subarray size, and so on
2. It iterates through each index of both the left and right subarrays, compares which is smaller, and stores the smaller one in the input array's index location
3. Now, if the left subarray is larger than the right subarray, then it stores the remaining elements of the left subarray in the input array
4. It does a similar thing if the right subarray is larger than the left subarray

 The snippet mentioned here is for sorting an array, but we can do the same with any kind of collection.

Understanding quick sort

Like merge sort, quick sort also sorts using the principle of divide and conquer—It also takes $O(n \log n)$ to do its job, but in the extreme worst case, it can take $O(n^2)$ to sort n elements (which is very rare). We can do this in place, so the memory used in quick sort is less.

How the quick sort algorithm works

The following gives a brief idea about how quick sort works:

1. It chooses an element called the `pivot` element
2. It divides the input collection into two sub-collections based on the `pivot` element
3. The division happens in a way that all elements in the left sub-collection are smaller than the `pivot` element, and all elements in the right sub-collection are larger than the `pivot` element
4. Now, the `pivot` element is at its proper place, so we freeze it
5. Repeat *step 1* to *step 4* until the sub-collection size becomes 0 or 1

Choosing the pivot element

There is no hard and fast rule for choosing the `pivot` element. Here are a few ways:

- Choose the first element as the `pivot` element
- Choose the last element as the `pivot` element
- Choose the middle element as the `pivot` element
- Choose a random element as the `pivot` element

The example we'll discuss here is to choose the last element as the `pivot` element.

Example based on quick sort

Let's use the same example as before to sort with quick sort:

Iteration 1:

17 12 29 21 5 7	Our input, `pivot` is 7
17 < 7	Ignore
12 < 7	Ignore
29 < 7	Ignore
21 < 7	Ignore
5 < 7	Swap 17 and 5 which gives 5 12 29 21 17 7
Swap the `pivot` element with the next index	5 7 29 21 17 12

Now, 7 is in sorted order.

Iteration 2:

5	last subarray has only one element, so sorted.

Iteration 3:

29 21 17 12	`pivot` is 12
29 < 12	Ignore
21 < 12	Ignore
17 < 12	Ignore
Swap the `pivot` element with the 0th index	12 21 17 29

Now, 12 is in sorted order.

Iteration 4:

21 17 29	`pivot` is 29
21 < 29	Swap the same index, so no change
17 < 29	Swap the same index, so no change
Swap the `pivot` element with the same index, so no change	21 17 29

Now, 29 is in sorted order.

Iteration 5:

21 17	`pivot` is 17
21 < 17	Ignore
Swap the `pivot` element with the 0th index	17 21

Now, 17 is in sorted order

Iteration 6:

21 is only one element in the sub-collection, so it's sorted.	Final output is 5 7 12 17 21 29

Implementing quick sort

Like merge sort, quick sort can be implemented with the help of two tasks. One is to call the sort API recursively by dividing the collection into sub-collections and the other task is to find the partition index from where the collection will be divided. So, here we have implemented those accordingly:

```
fun <E: Comparable<E>> Array<E>.sort() {
    sort(this, 0, size - 1)
}

private fun <E: Comparable<E>> sort(arr: Array<E>, low: Int, high: Int) {
    if (low < high) {
        val partitionIndex = partition(arr, low, high)

        sort(arr, low, partitionIndex - 1)
        sort(arr, partitionIndex + 1, high)
    }
}
```

The `sort()` API is the public function exposed to the outside world that calls the private `sort(...)` function with the lower and upper index of the collection. The private `sort(...)` function recursively calls itself by partitioning the input collection into two. This process happens until the sub-collections have only one element (that is, *size = 1*). Let's see how the partitioning happens:

```
private fun <E: Comparable<E>> partition(arr: Array<E>, low: Int, high: Int): Int {
    val pivot = arr[high]
    var i = low - 1
    for (j in low until high) {
        if (arr[j] <= pivot) {
            i++
            arr[i] = arr[j].also { arr[j] = arr[i] }
        }
    }
    arr[i + 1] = arr[high].also { arr[high] = arr[i + 1] }
    return i + 1;
}
```

Here is a step-by-step guide to the preceding code snippet:

1. We choose the last element as the `pivot` element.
2. The, we initiate a `temp` index with `low - 1`. This index indicates the position at which all the elements smaller than the `pivot` element should be swapped.

3. Compare every element of the collection with the `pivot` one.
4. If smaller, increment the index created at *step 2* and swap those two elements.
5. At the end, we know the final index of the `pivot` element, so swap that indexed element with the `pivot` element.

Understanding heap sort

Heap sort can be imagined as an improved version of selection sort. Like selection sort, this also has two sub-collections (a sorted one and an unsorted one). Initially, the unsorted sub-collection is the input collection, whereas the sorted sub-collection is empty. During the process, it tries to remove elements one by one from the unsorted sub-collection and adds them into the sorted sub-collection. Though the concept of sorting is similar to selection sort, the way it does it's different from selection sort. Its performance is *O(n log n)*.

A basic introduction to heap

We know that heap sort is based on the heap data structure, so it's wise to have a basic understanding of heap data structure before we actually move into heap sort. We are not going to discuss it fully; instead, we'll just get an overview of related concepts with respect to heap sort.

Binary heap

A binary heap can be defined as a special **complete binary tree**. Now the question is what is a complete binary tree? To answer this, we can say that it's a binary tree the(parent can have a maximum of two children) in which every level must be complete (except the last one).

The difference between a complete binary tree and a binary heap is that in a binary heap, the elements are sorted in a special manner. In this case, each parent element is either larger than both of its children (called a **max heap**) or smaller than both of its children (called a **min heap**).

The best thing about a binary heap is that it can be represented either in an array or a tree, because it's a complete binary tree. The example we'll see here represents the binary heap using an array. If the parent is at the ith index, then the left node is at index *2 * i + 1* and the right node is at index *2 * i + 2*.

How the heap sort algorithm works

So far, we have understood the basics of the heap, so now, let's see how we can use it to write the heap sort algorithm. Here is the way it works:

1. It creates a max heap from the input collection.
2. Now, we know that the largest element is at the root of the heap, so swap it with the last element of the heap.
3. Reduce the heap size by 1 by removing the last element (the largest one) from the heap. Now, that element is at its proper index.
4. Repeat the preceding steps until the heap size becomes one.

Let's consider the same example and sort it using heap sort.

Iteration 1:

17 12 29 21 5 7	Our input

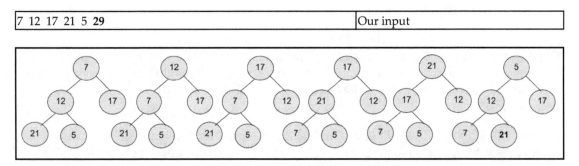

The index of **29** is last, so remove it from the heap and move to the next iteration.

Iteration 2:

7 12 17 21 5 **29**	Our input

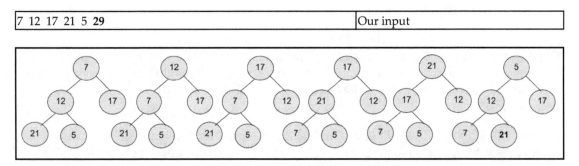

The index of **21** is last, so remove it from the heap and move to the next iteration.

Iteration 3:

5 12 17 7 **21 29**	Our input

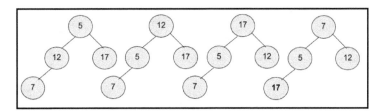

The index of **17** is last, so remove it from the heap and move to the next iteration.

Iteration 4:

7 5 12 **17 21 29**	Our input

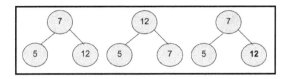

The index of **12** is last, so remove it from the heap and move to the next iteration.

Iteration 5:

7 5 **12 17 21 29**	Our input

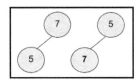

The index of **7** is last, so remove it from the heap and move to the next iteration.

Iteration 6:

5 7 **12 17 21 29**	Our input

Now the heap has only one element, 5, so it's all sorted. So, the final output after the sorting is **5   7   12   17   21   29**.

Implementing heap sort

We have implemented heap sort by exposing the `sort()` API to the outside world. Here is the implementation:

```
fun <E: Comparable<E>> Array<E>.sort() {
    val middle = size / 2 - 1
    for (i in middle downTo 0) {
        heapify(this, size, i)
    }
    for (i in size - 1 downTo 0) {
        this[0] = this[i].also { this[i] = this[0] }
        heapify(this, i, 0)
    }
}
```

In the first `for` loop, we build the `max heap` by rearranging the input collection. Once the heap is built, we know that that the largest element is at the 0th index of the collection (that is, the root of the heap). So, in the second `for` loop, we swap the 0th index with the last index of the unsorted sub-collection and then rebuild the heap with one less element. Building the heap is done with the `heapify` function. The following code snippet is its implementation:

```
private fun <E: Comparable<E>> heapify(arr: Array<E>, heapSize: Int, root:
Int) {
    var largest = root
    val leftNode = 2 * root + 1
    val rightNode = 2 * root + 2
    if (leftNode < heapSize && arr[leftNode] > arr[largest]) largest =
leftNode
    if (rightNode < heapSize && arr[rightNode] > arr[largest]) largest =
rightNode

    if (largest != root) {
        arr[root] = arr[largest].also { arr[largest] = arr[root] }
        heapify(arr, heapSize, largest)
    }
}
```

Here is a step-by-step guide to the `heapify` function:

1. Consider the root as the largest element.
2. Get the indexes of both the left and right children of the heap.
3. Compare them with the parent, and if a smaller one is found, then swap that child with the parent.

4. Check whether the elements before and after the swap are the same or not. If they're not the same, swap those two elements and build the heap again by calling `heapify` recursively.

Summary

Though we have tried to cover many commonly used sorting algorithms, this is not the end of all sorting algorithms. There are many other algorithms that are not covered in this book and are open for you to explore.

Out of all the algorithms discussed here, the following table gives a nice comparison of their performance:

Algorithm	Performance
Bubble sort	$O(n^2)$
Selection sort	$O(n^2)$
Insertion sort	$O(n^2)$
Merge sort	$O(n \log n)$
Quick sort	$O(n \log n)$ in worst $O(n^2)$
Heap sort	$O(n \log n)$

Now, you might have a better understanding of which sorting algorithm to choose, and when.

Questions

1. Implement Quick Sort in descending order.
2. Implement all the sorting algorithms discussed above for immutable list.

Section 4: Modern and Advanced Data Structures

4

This section walks you through modern programming techniques and their requisite data structures. You will learn about the Collections framework in Kotlin, which provides you with some pre-built data structures, including Maps, Lists, and Set, thereby increasing your productivity as you no longer need to create your custom data structures for every program you write. You will also learn about functional programming and its associated data structures, such as Type Constructors, Monads, and Functors.

The following chapters will be covered in this section:

- Chapter 8, *Collections and Data Operations in Kotlin*
- Chapter 9, *Introduction to Functional Programming*

8
Collections and Data Operations in Kotlin

In Chapter 7, *Understanding Sorting Algorithms*, we dealt a lot with arrays, lists, maps, and other data structures, and we created our custom implementations of them. Thankfully, Kotlin provides you with a wide range of predefined collection data structures for you under the umbrella of the collections framework.

In this chapter, we are going to discuss the collections framework and data operations in Kotlin. Kotlin inherited the collections framework from Java but has made significant improvements to it, making it easier for developers to use the collections framework while applying functional programming constructs.

The collections framework that Kotlin provides is more functional (functional as in functional programming) than Java, and is easier to use and understand.

We will start this chapter with some fundamentals of collections and will gradually move on to the data operations and functional constructs that the collections framework supports in Kotlin.

This chapter will cover the following topics:

- Introduction to collections
- Understanding a group of ordered elements—`List`, `MutableList`
- Group of Unique Elements—`Set`, `MutableSet`
- The key-value pairs—`Map`, `MutableMap`
- Data operations in collection—`map`, `filter`, `flatMap`, `drop`, `take`, `zip`, and so on

So, what are we waiting for? Let's get started with collections.

Technical requirements

The following technologies are used in this chapter:

- Kotlin language
- IntelliJ IDEA
- Gradle build environment

We are assuming that you've gone through the earlier chapters of the book, and are thus familiar with the following:

- Basic idioms and syntax of the Kotlin language
- Concepts of basic data structures, such as lists, sets, maps, and so on

The GitHub URL for the chapter can be found at `https://github.com/PacktPublishing/ Hands-On-Data-Structures-and-Algorithms-with-Kotlin/tree/master/Chapter08`.

Introduction to collections

In programming, the word "framework" generally refers to a structure underlying a system that can be used within the system to perform a set of similar operations. Thus, we can think of a framework as a collection of libraries/APIs.

Similarly, the collections framework provides developers with a set of APIs to perform common data/data structure-related operations (which can be called **data operations**). The collections framework contains a few of the most commonly needed interfaces to deal with data structures and their common concrete implementations. You can always create your own custom implementation of a `Collection` interface. The collections framework also defines the most common algorithms, including the following:

- Searching
- Sorting
- Insertion
- Deletion
- Manipulation

All the lists, maps, and sets we use in our programs every day are part of this collections framework.

All collections frameworks contain the following:

- **Interfaces**: The collections framework defines a set of interfaces for different data structures, along with common methods for different data operations. These interfaces can be implemented with custom logic for those data operations. Some examples are `List`, `Map`, `Set` , and so on.

- **Implementations**: In addition to ready-to-implement interfaces, the collection framework also provides a set of concrete classes that implement those interfaces with most common algorithms for data operations. These concrete classes are often not optimized (as the definition of optimization may change from project to project, based on requirements), but they serve a great purpose of common requirements. A few examples are `ArrayList`, `HashMap`, `HashSet`, and so on.

- **Algorithms**: These are the methods that carry out useful computations, such as sorting and searching on objects. These objects are the ones that implement collection interfaces. These algorithms are polymorphic, which means that the same method can be applied to other different implementations of the desired collections interface. So to sum up, algorithms are a reusable functionality.

Apart from the Java and Kotlin collection frameworks, some popular examples are the C++ **Standard Template Library** (**STL**) and Smalltalk's collection hierarchy.

Benefits of a collections framework

So, what are the advantages of having a collections framework? There are several, but most importantly, it reduces programming efforts and time, and increases compatibility between APIs. The collections framework provides a developer with high-quality (in terms of performance and code optimization) implementations of useful data structures and algorithms, while facilitating you with interoperability between unrelated APIs. You can use these implementations in your program, thus reducing your programming effort and time.

For example, in previous chapters, we have worked with arrays, lists, and maps. We've already seen how complex it is to define your own data structures. All that complexity can be avoided by using the collections framework.

Moreover, the collections framework in Java and Kotlin contains predefined common sorting and searching algorithms (for common data types, such as `String`, `Int`, `Long`, and so on; for custom classes/data types, you've to define your own), thus relieving you further.

The collection framework hierarchy

So, as we have now been introduced to the collections framework, let's have a look at the hierarchy of classes and interfaces in the collection framework in Kotlin.

So, let's go through the following diagram:

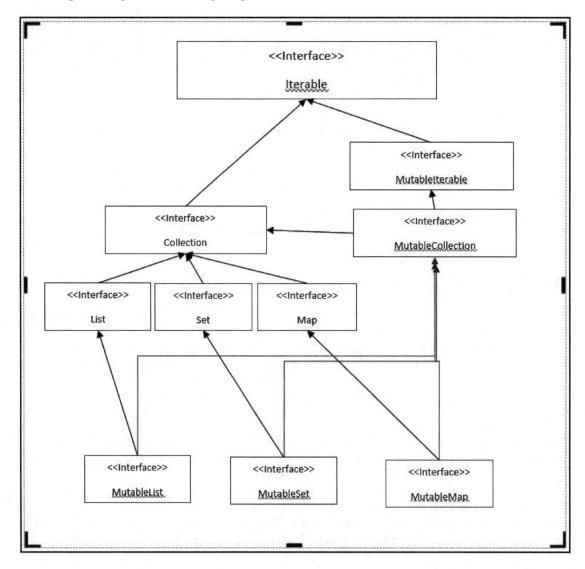

As we mentioned previously, the collections framework is a set of data types and classes that let us work with a group (or groups) of data. That group may be in the form of a simple `List`/`Map`/`Set` or any other data structure.

The preceding diagram represents the collections framework of Kotlin. Just like Java, all `Collection` interfaces in Kotlin, are originated from the `Iterable` interface. However, the Kotlin collections framework is a bit different than that of Java, as Kotlin distinguishes between mutable and immutable collections.

Kotlin has two base `Collection` interfaces, namely `Iterable` and `MutableIterable`. The `Iterable` interface is extended by the `Collection` interface, which defines basic read-only collection operations (such as `size`, `isEmpty()`, `contains()`, and so on).

The `MutableCollection` interface extends the `Collection` interface and the `MutableIterable` interface, adding the read/write feature.

 The collection framework was introduced in Java before the formation of the Kotlin language, and it was included in Kotlin from the very beginning.

But aren't you curious about why there are so many collection types? Let's look at the purpose of some of the most commonly used collection types.

Understanding a group of ordered elements – List, MutableList

`List` is one of the most commonly used collection data types. It is an implementation of the collection to work with a group of ordered data.

 The data in a list may be ordered based on when it was added (for example if we add 3 after 4 to an `Int` list, then 4 will appear in the list before 3, much like an array) or we may even ordered them with ordering/sorting algorithms.

The following is a list of the most important functions defined in the `List` interface:

- `fun get(index: Int):E`: This method is used to get an element from the list at the given index.

- `fun indexOf(element: @UnsafeVariance E):Int`: This method is useful to identify the index of an element in the list. This method should search for the specified element inside the whole list and should return the position of the element if it's in the list; it would return -1 otherwise.
- `fun listIterator(): ListIterator<E>`: This method is used if you want to get an instance of `ListIterator` (covered later in this chapter while covering `Iterator` and `Iterable`)
- `fun subList(fromIndex: Int, toIndex: Int): List<E>`: This returns a portion of the list with the specified `fromIndex` and `toIndex`.

You may be wondering, if it contains only the read-only functions, then how do you have a list with data? While you cannot put data to an immutable list after it has been created, you can definitely create an immutable list with pre-populated data (obviously, otherwise there wouldn't be any purpose of having immutable lists). You can achieve that in many ways, but the most popular one is to use the `listOf` function.

The `listOf` function declaration looks like the following (it can be found inside `Collections.kt`, in the `kotlin.collections` package):

```
public fun <T> listOf(vararg elements: T): List<T>
```

As we can see in the function declaration, the function takes a `vararg` parameter of a generic type as elements. The function would return a `List` instance containing those elements. As you already know, the significance of a `vararg` argument is that it can contain 0 to almost 64 K (if each argument is of 1 byte, a function can have maximum 64 K bytes allocation, so actually it would be less) arguments within it; so, while creating a list with the `listOf` function, you can call it even without parameters to create an empty list, or call it with as many arguments as you need (assuming you wouldn't need beyond the 64 K bytes limit) to create the read-only list with them.

The following program is an example of the `listOf` function:

```kotlin
fun main(args: Array<String>) {
    val list = listOf(10, 8, 18, 45, 63, 49, 88, 15, 62)
    val linkedList = LinkedList<Int>(list)

    for (i in linkedList) {
        println("List Item $i")
    }
}
```

The preceding program was a simple one. We just created a List of Int containing random numbers (hardcoded). We then created a LinkedList from this list and then used a for loop to loop through and print all the numbers in the list.

Simple and straightforward enough, isn't it? As we have already created our custom implementations of LinkedList, just compare that code with this one, which is so simple and compact. That's the true benefit of the collections framework.

The output is as follows:

```
"C:\Program Files\Java\jdk1.8.0_131\bin\java" ...
List Item 10
List Item 8
List Item 18
List Item 45
List Item 63
List Item 49
List Item 88
List Item 15
List Item 62


Process finished with exit code 0
```

So, we successfully created a LinkedList and looped through it. Now, what about sorting it?

Various operations (sorting, searching) on List

Let's modify the previous program, and add the following just before the loop:

```
linkedList.sort()
```

This single statement will be enough to sort the `List` in ascending order. The following is the output:

```
"C:\Program Files\Java\jdk1.8.0_131\bin\java" ...
List Item 8
List Item 10
List Item 15
List Item 18
List Item 45
List Item 49
List Item 62
List Item 63
List Item 88

Process finished with exit code 0
```

But, for all these operations, do we really require `LinkedList`? The answer is no. We've already learned about the significance of `LinkedList` and in which scenarios it is most useful. We could've easily achieved the preceding examples without `LinkedList`. To be more truthful, the Kotlin collections framework (`kotlin.collections`) doesn't even contain `LinkedList`; it's derived from the `java.util` package.

So, we can easily re-write the preceding program as follows:

```
fun main(args: Array<String>) {
    val list = listOf(10, 8, 18, 45, 63, 49, 88, 15, 62)

    val sortedList = list.sorted()

    for (i in sortedList) {
        println("List Item $i")
    }
}
```

The preceding program is almost similar to the previous one. The output is also the same. The only difference here is that, instead of using `LinkedList`, we used `List` only from the `kotlin.collections` package.

There's another difference as well. In the example with `LinkedList`, we sorted the original list, but here, if you look closely, you can identify that we are storing the sorted list into another variable, rather than sorting the original one. The reason? It's quite simple; we cannot modify an immutable list once created, so calling the `sorted()` function on an immutable list will get you a new list instance with sorted elements.

In simpler words, `LinkedList` is a mutable collection, as it comes from Java, and in Java there's no concrete concept of immutable collections. All implementations of the collections framework in Java are mutable. But in Kotlin, the collections framework differentiates between mutable and immutable collections. We don't always have to modify an existing collection, do we? It's always better practice to use immutable collections in your Kotlin code (with other languages, as well, if available).

Sorting a list with custom class / data types

You're probably thinking of how to sort a list with custom classes/data types? Let's do it.

The following is a custom class that we're going to use:

```
data class Employee(
        val employeeID: Int,
        val employeeName: String
)
```

It's a simple data class representing an employee with employee ID and name, so let's create a list of employees, as follows:

```
val employeeList = listOf(
                Employee(2, "Chandra Sekhar Nayak"),
                Employee(1, "Rivu Chakraborty"),
                Employee(4, "Indranil Dutta"),
                Employee(3, "Sonkho Deep Mondal"),
                Employee(6, "Debraj Dey"),
                Employee(5, "Koushik Mridha")
)
```

We're going to sort them with their respective `employeeID` and then we will print them. The following is the complete program:

```
fun main(args: Array<String>) {
    val employeeList = listOf(
                Employee(2, "Chandra Sekhar Nayak"),
                Employee(1, "Rivu Chakraborty"),
                Employee(4, "Indranil Dutta"),
                Employee(3, "Sonkho Deep Mondal"),
                Employee(6, "Debraj Dey"),
                Employee(5, "Koushik Mridha")
    )

    val sortedEmpList = employeeList.sortedWith(Comparator { e1, e2 ->
        when {
            e1?.employeeID ?: 0 <= e2?.employeeID ?: 0 -> -1
```

```
                    e1?.employeeID ?: 0 == e2?.employeeID ?: 0 -> 0
                    else -> 1
            }
    })

    for (employee in sortedEmpList) {
        println(employee)
    }
}
```

So, we used the `sortedWith` function instead of `sorted()`. This function requires an instance of `Comparator` to be passed. `Comparator` is an interface, which has a function calleed `compare`.

While implementing `Comparator` for your custom data type / class, you should override `compare`. The `compare` function is called with two instances of your custom class/data type. You should return a negative value if the first one is less than the second one, 0, if both of them should be equal, and a positive value if the first one is greater than the second one.

The output is as follows:

```
"C:\Program Files\Java\jdk1.8.0_131\bin\java" ...
Employee(employeeID=1, employeeName=Rivu Chakraborty)
Employee(employeeID=2, employeeName=Chandra Sekhar Nayak)
Employee(employeeID=3, employeeName=Sonkho Deep Mondal)
Employee(employeeID=4, employeeName=Indranil Dutta)
Employee(employeeID=5, employeeName=Koushik Mridha)
Employee(employeeID=6, employeeName=Debraj Dey)

Process finished with exit code 0
```

Quite handy, isn't it? However, the Kotlin collections API provides you with a better and functional way to achieve the same.

Have a look at the the following code:

```
employeeList.sortedBy {
    it.employeeID
}.forEach {
    println(it)
}
```

This code block effectively does the same as the previous one, but, in a functional way.

The `sortedBy` operator takes a lambda, which should return a comparable value based on which sorting operation should be performed.

The following is the declaration of the `sortedBy` operator:

```
inline fun <T, R : Comparable<R>> Iterable<T>.sortedBy (crossinline
selector: (T) -> R?): List<T>
```

So, as mentioned, `sortedBy` expects a lambda to return an instance of `Comparable`, in order to compare and sort the resultant list. `Comparable` is a Kotlin interface that has a function called `compareTo`, and every built-in data type in Kotlin has this implementation.

Searching collections

While we've discovered various ways of sorting a collection/list with ease, the collections API also makes it easy for searching an element from a list.

The following is an example:

```
fun main(args: Array<String>) {
    val list = listOf(10, 8, 18, 45, 63, 49, 88, 15, 62)
    println("Index of 18 ${list.binarySearch(18)}")
}
```

So, we created a `list` and searched for `18` in that `list`.

The output is as follows:

```
Index of 18 2

Process finished with exit code 0
```

Mutable lists

So, we've seen how to work with immutable lists with pre-defined elements, but what if we need to add items to the `list` dynamically? Kotlin provides you with mutable lists for this purpose.

The following example will help you understand mutable lists:

```
fun main(args: Array<String>) {
    val list = mutableListOf(1, 2, 5)
```

```kotlin
    println("-----Created With Items-----")
    for (i in list) {
        println("list item $i")
    }

    //Adding Items

    list.add(6)          // (1)
    list.add(2, 3)       // (2)
    list.add(3, 4)       // (3)

    println("-----After Adding Items-----")
    for (i in list) {
        println("list item $i")
    }
}
```

Here, we created a list with the `mutableListOf()` function, which lets you create a mutable list with specified items and/or data types.

In comments 1, 2, and 3, we added items to the list. While adding items to the list, it generally appends the list; that is, items are generally added to the list, unless you specify a position where to place the item in the list. We did the same in comments 2 and 3; we specified to add the item 3 on the index (position, starting from 0) 2 and item 4 to index 3, while pushing the already existing items to the next indexes.

The output is as follows:

```
"C:\Program Files\Java\jdk1.8.0_131\bin\java" ...
-----Created With Items-----
list item 1
list item 2
list item 5
-----After Adding Items-----
list item 1
list item 2
list item 3
list item 4
list item 5
list item 6

Process finished with exit code 0
```

Again, quite easy and handy, isn't it?

For `listOf` or any other collections function as well, type inference is there, so there is no need to specify the generic type of the collection. The type of the elements passed inside the function becomes the type of the collection.

So far, we've accessed a whole list and added items, but what about modifying/accessing a single item from the list? Let's look at an example:

```
fun main(args: Array<String>) {
    val list = mutableListOf(1, 2, 3, 0, 5, 6, 7, 8)

    list[3] = 4
    println("3rd and 4th Item on List -> ${list[3]}, ${list.get(4)}")
}
```

In the preceding example, we've created a `list`, and then modified the third item (counting from 0), which was 0 earlier. We then printed the third and fourth items.

The output is as follows:

```
"C:\Program Files\Java\jdk1.8.0_131\bin\java" ...
3rd and 4th Item on List -> 4, 5


Process finished with exit code 0
```

So, we got a grip on lists. Didn't we? Let's move forward with another collection type—sets.

Group of unique elements – Set, MutableSet

`Set` also has two variants in Kotlin, like `List` or any other collection—`Set` and `MutableSet`. Like `List`, `Set` is read-only and `MutableList` and `MutableSet` are the mutable versions of `Set`, which contain the read/write functionalities.

As with `List`, `Set` also has read-only properties and functions, such as `size`, `isEmpty()`, `get(index: Int)`, and so on. We are not describing them here again to avoid redundant contents in this book. The big difference between `Set` and `List` is that, `Set` doesn't do ordering like `List` (unless you use `OrderedSet`), so it lacks the functions that involve orders, such as `indexOf(item)`, `add(index, item)`, and so on.

`Set`, as you already know from earlier chapters, represents mathematical sets (the ones in `Set` theory).

From previous chapters, you already know that we cannot put duplicate items in sets. If you put an item multiple times in a `Set`, the `Set` will keep the item only once and will ignore the rest. In earlier chapters, you've already learned how to achieve this behavior while creating your custom sets. Thankfully, the Kotlin collections framework contains `Set` implementations, so that you don't have to create your custom one anymore.

 To avoid redundancy, we skipped mentioning MutableSet and Immutable Sets separately. Instead, we're showing an example of MutableSet directly, which is identical to that of `List`.

The following is an example for you:

```
fun main(args: Array<String>) {
    val set = mutableSetOf(1, 2, 3, 4, 4, 1,2)

    println("set before add $set")

    set.add(4)
    set.add(5)
    set.add(5)
    set.add(6)

    println("set after add $set")
}
```

The output is as follows:

```
"C:\Program Files\Java\jdk1.8.0_131\bin\java" ...
set before add [1, 2, 3, 4]
set after add [1, 2, 3, 4, 5, 6]

Process finished with exit code 0
```

So, `Set` elegantly refused to keep duplicate items. But, with `Int`, what will happen if we use a custom data type/class? Just have a look at the following program:

```
data class MyDataClass (val someNumericValue:Int, val
someStringValue:String)

fun main(args: Array<String>) {
    val dataClassSet = setOf(
            MyDataClass(1, "1st obj"),
            MyDataClass(2, "2nd obj"),
            MyDataClass(3, "3rd obj"),
```

```
            MyDataClass(2, "2nd obj"),
            MyDataClass(4, "4th obj"),
            MyDataClass(5, "5th obj"),
            MyDataClass(2, "will be added"),
            MyDataClass(3, "3rd obj")
    )

    println("Printing items of dataClassSet one by one")
    for(item in dataClassSet) {
        println(item)
    }
}
```

So, we used a data class for creating our own class / custom data type.

The output is as follows:

```
"C:\Program Files\Java\jdk1.8.0_131\bin\java" ...
Printing items of dataClassSet one by one
MyDataClass(someNumericValue=1, someStringValue=1st obj)
MyDataClass(someNumericValue=2, someStringValue=2nd obj)
MyDataClass(someNumericValue=3, someStringValue=3rd obj)
MyDataClass(someNumericValue=4, someStringValue=4th obj)
MyDataClass(someNumericValue=5, someStringValue=5th obj)
MyDataClass(someNumericValue=2, someStringValue=will be added)


Process finished with exit code 0
```

The reason, we used a data class instead of a normal class is that with data classes, you don't need to have custom implementations of methods such as toString(), hash(), and equals(), which are required by Set for equality checking.

So, we're done with List and Set. Let's move on with Map.

Maps – working with key-value pairs

The Map interface is a bit different than all the other interfaces in the collections framework, such as Set or List. Unlike them, it works with key-value pairs. If you're thinking of Pair, then let me say no, this is not similar to Pair. A Pair is just a pair of two values combined together while a Map is a collection of key-value pairs.

In a `Map`, keys are unique and cannot be duplicated, whereas values can be redundant. If you try to add two values with the same key, then the latter one will replace the previous one. Values, on the other hand, can be redundant/duplicate. The main reason behind this behavior is that in `Map`, items are not stored based on order or anything else, but rather a value is stored and retrieved with respect to its key, so redundant keys will make it impossible to distinguish them from each other and to fetch their value. That's the only reason a `Map` is called a key-value pair. If you can recall Chapter 5, *Maps – Working with Key-Value Pairs*, then you will be able to easily identify that the `Map` interface is the exact program representation of the `Map` data structure.

The declaration of `Map` in Kotlin reads like the `Map<K, out V>`. The `K` is the generic type of the key and the `V` is the generic type of the value.

To learn more about collections, let's have a look at a few of the functions and properties. Go through the following list:

- `val size: Int`: Indicates the size of the `Map`; that is,the number of key-value pairs residing inside the `Map`.
- `fun isEmpty(): Boolean`: This function helps in checking whether a `Map` is empty or not.
- `fun containsKey(key: K): Boolean`: This function checks for the provided key inside the collection of key-value pairs and it has and returns `true` if found.
- `operator fun get(key: K): V?`: This function cum operator (if used by square brackets `[]` like an array) returns the value corresponding to a key or null if the key doesn't exist within it.
- `val keys: Set<K>`: Indicates the collection of keys available in the `Map` at a point of time. As keys cannot be duplicate and they are not ordered, a `Set` is the best data structure to hold them.
- `val values: Collection<V>`: Contains all the values of the `Map` as a collection.
- `interface Entry<out K, out V>`: Defined inside the `Map` interface. An `Entry` represents a single key-value pair in the `Map`. They key-value pairs are stored as an entry inside the `Map`.
- `val entries: Set<Map.Entry<K, V>>`: Gets you all the entries in the `Map`.

The aforementioned were read-only interfaces of Map, as it only supports read-only operations. For read/write access, you have to use the MutableMap. So, let us now have a look at the read/write interfaces provided by MutableMap:

- fun put(key: K, value: V): V?: Adds a key-value pair to the Map and returns the previous value associated with the key (if any, or null if the key wasn't present in the Map earlier).
- fun remove(key: K): V?: Removes a key-value pair from the map with the key and returns the value. It returns null if the key doesn't exist in the Map.
- fun putAll(from: Map<out K, V>): Unit: Adds the key-value pairs from the provided map.
- fun clear(): Unit: As the name suggests, it clears the map, It removes everything that the map contains: every key and every value.

So, as we got to learn about the interfaces and functions the Map interfaces has to offer, let's now look at an example with Map. Go through the following code:

```
fun main(args: Array<String>) {
    val map = mapOf(
            "Key One" to 1.0f,
            "Key Two" to 2.0f,
            "Key Three" to 3.0f,
            "Key Four" to 4.0f,
            "Key Five" to 5.0f,
            "Key Six" to 0.0f,      // (1)
            "Key Six" to 6.0f       // (2)
            )

    println("The value at Key `Key Four` is ${map["Key Four"]}")

    println("Contents in map")
    for(entry in map) {
        println("Key ${entry.key}, Value ${entry.value}")
    }

    val mutableMap = map.toMutableMap()

    println("Replacing value at key - `Key Five` - ${mutableMap.put("Key Five",5.5f)}")     // (3)

    println("Contents in mutableMap")
    for(entry in mutableMap) {
        println("Key ${entry.key}, Value ${entry.value}")
    }
}
```

Before explaining the program, let's have a look at the output:

```
The value at Key `Key Four` is 4.0
Contents in map
Key Key One, Value 1.0
Key Key Two, Value 2.0
Key Key Three, Value 3.0
Key Key Four, Value 4.0
Key Key Five, Value 5.0
Key Key Six, Value 6.0
Replacing value at key - `Key Five` - 5.0
Contents in mutableMap
Key Key One, Value 1.0
Key Key Two, Value 2.0
Key Key Three, Value 3.0
Key Key Four, Value 4.0
Key Key Five, Value 5.5
Key Key Six, Value 6.0


Process finished with exit code 0
```

The preceding program was quite straightforward. We created a `Map` and then printed all the contents. We then created a `MutableMap` from that `map` and replaced the content with keys,`"Key Five"`, and again printed them.

So, we demonstrated the use of two types of maps here—the read-only `Map` and read/write `MutableMap`.

Kotlin provides you with a version of the `mapOf()` function that accepts `vararg` parameters of type `Pair`. This makes it easy for you to create read-only maps—just pass the key-value pairs as the instances of `Pair` to the `mapOf()` function.

While creating the `map`, on comment (1), we passed `Pair`, `"Key Six"` to `0.0f` and on comment (2), we passed the pair `"Key Six"` to `6.0F` to the same `mapOf` function, to check which value the `map` stores for the key,`"Key Six"`. The output suggests that the `map` took the second one,`6.0F`, as we described earlier that a `map` always takes the last value for the same key.

Also note that Kotlin supports arrays like square brackets in `Map` as well. Instead of the index, you can pass here the key.

So, as we got our hands dirty with three of the most important interfaces in the Kotlin collections framework, `List`, `Set`, and `Map`, let's now move forward and get ourselves introduced to data operations in collections.

Understanding data operations in collections

The Kotlin collections framework is full of interesting features that make it stand apart from the collections frameworks in other languages, such as Java. You already been introduced to some of those features, such as separate interfaces for read-only and mutable collections, square box operator, such as arrays, and so on. What I'm going to introduce now is probably the most interesting feature of the Kotlin collections framework—data operation (extension) functions.

Kotlin supports data operation (extension) functions for all of its collections framework interfaces. Now, what are data operation functions? They are extension functions by which we can access/process or operate on data from a collection. If you are familiar with the ReactiveX framework (for example, RxJava or RxKotlin) or any of the Reactive streams framework, you'll find it similar, as Kotlin picked them mostly from there.

The following is a list of some of the collection data operation functions that we are going to cover here:

- The `map` function (functor)
- The `filter` function
- The `flatMap` function (`monad`)
- The `drop` functions
- The `take` functions
- The `zip` functions

So, what are we waiting for? Let's get started.

Although the data operation functions with collections make you feel like you are working with streams /Rx, they are nowhere similar to streams/Rx. What they do is simply use higher-order functions and extension functions to provide you with stream- like interfaces and internally they operate on the same loops. (Yes, you read it right; they use loops to produce results and then return them from the function just like a simple imperial program.).It is advisable to avoid chains of these functions in your program, as you'll end up with multiple loops. Using forEach or your own loop in such scenarios is a better choice as you will be able to perform multiple operation with single loop with forEach or with your own loop. However, for a single operation, you can definitely use these functions to make your code well organized.

The map function

The map function (or the functor in FP) is one of the most useful data operation functions. It helps you enormously to write well-organized code while avoiding loops (although it'll internally use loops, you're set free from writing those boilerplates and can focus only on your logic) to perform the same action on each element of the collection or transform each element of the collection.

The map function returns a result List by applying the transform function on each element of the collection on which it is called. The transform function is nothing but a lambda you want to be executed for each element of the collection.

To explain it more precisely, if a collection has N number of elements, the map function would call the transform function N times, with each of those elements passed as parameter in each call. The map function then performs the required computation on the elements and should return the resultant item, which should be placed in the resultant collection, in place of the passed item.

The following is an example of the map function:

```
fun main(args: Array<String>) {
    val list = listOf<Int>(1, 2, 3, 4, 5, 6, 7, 8, 9, 10)

    println("modifiedList -> ${list.map { it + 3 }}")
}
```

So, we had a list of Int. We needed to add each item from the list with 3, and we did this with ease with just a single line of code, list.map { it + 3 }, which would normally take us two-three lines more of boilerplate. Insane, isn't it?

The output is as follows:

```
"C:\Program Files\Java\jdk1.8.0_131\bin\java" ...
modifiedList -> [4, 5, 6, 7, 8, 9, 10, 11, 12, 13]

Process finished with exit code 0
```

The filter function

Have you ever heard of the phrase *finding a needle in a bag of sand*? While writing our code, we often face similar situations. We can often stumble at a need to filter out a small amount of data from a huge collection. Without the Kotlin collections framework, you would probably have to write a lot of KLOC. Not any more; the `filter` function is here to save your day.

The lambda in the `filter` function would be called for each item of the collection as a separate iteration and should return `true` or `false`. Based on the lambda's result, it is determined whether the passed item should be on the resultant `list` or not.

The following is an example:

```kotlin
fun main(args: Array<String>) {
    val list = 1.until(50).toList()

    println("Filtered List with Even Numbers-> ${list.filter { it % 2 == 0 }}")

    val filteredList = list.filter {
        val sqroot = sqrt(it.toDouble()).roundToInt()
        sqroot * sqroot == it
    }

    println("Filtered List with Perfect Squares -> $filteredList")
}
```

How long would a program be if you need to implement custom filtering logic to filter only square roots from a list of integers? That's right; in the preceding program, we accomplished the same with just three lines, all thanks to the `filter` function.

The following output is as expected:

```
"C:\Program Files\Java\jdk1.8.0_131\bin\java" ...
Filtered List with Even Numbers-> [2, 4, 6, 8, 10,
 12, 14, 16, 18, 20, 22, 24, 26, 28, 30, 32, 34, 36,
 38, 40, 42, 44, 46, 48]
Filtered List with Perfect Squares -> [1, 4, 9, 16,
 25, 36, 49]

Process finished with exit code 0
```

The flatMap function

The `flatMap` function (or the `monad`, explained in `Chapter 9`, *Introduction to Functional Programming*), is another great FP feature offered by the Kotlin collections framework.

Just like the `map` function, the lambda in the `flatMap` receives each of the items in the collection as an iteration, but unlike the lambda in the `map` function, where it returns the raw values, the lambda in `flatMap` must return another instance of the collection (of the same type; that is, another `List` for `flatMap` on `List`) for each of the items passed. These returned collection instances are then flattened to create the resultant collection:

```
fun main(args: Array<String>) {
    val list = listOf(10, 20, 30)
    println("flatMappedList -> ${
        list.flatMap {
            it.rangeTo(it * 2).toList()
        }
    }")
}
```

The output is as follows:

```
"C:\Program Files\Java\jdk1.8.0_131\bin\java" ...
flatMappedList -> [10, 11, 12, 13, 14, 15, 16, 17,
 18, 19, 20, 20, 21, 22, 23, 24, 25, 26, 27, 28, 29,
 30, 31, 32, 33, 34, 35, 36, 37, 38, 39, 40, 30, 31,
 32, 33, 34, 35, 36, 37, 38, 39, 40, 41, 42, 43, 44,
 45, 46, 47, 48, 49, 50, 51, 52, 53, 54, 55, 56, 57,
 58, 59, 60]

Process finished with exit code 0
```

For each element (10, 20, and 30), it created a `List` of elements:

```
10 -> 10, 11, 12, .........., 19, 20
20 -> 20, 21, 22, ........, 39, 40
30 -> 30, 31, 32, ........., 59, 60
```

The drop functions

There may be some scenarios when you want to drop a portion (say the first five or last ten) of the collection and work on those remaining. The Kotlin collections framework provides you with a set of `drop` functions that can help you in these scenarios. Have a look at the following program:

```
fun main(args: Array<String>) {
    val list = 1.until(50).toList()

    println("list.drop(20) -> ${list.drop(20)}")             //(1)
    println("list.dropLast(20) -> ${list.dropLast(20)}")     //(2)
}
```

In the preceding program, we've dropped the first 20 items from the `list` on comment 1, and on comment 2, we've dropped the last 20 items. The `drop` function drops the first N numbers from a collection, whereas `dropLast` drops the last N numbers from the collection.

The output is as follows:

```
"C:\Program Files\Java\jdk1.8.0_131\bin\java" ...
list.drop(20) -> [21, 22, 23, 24, 25, 26, 27, 28, 29,
 30, 31, 32, 33, 34, 35, 36, 37, 38, 39, 40, 41, 42,
 43, 44, 45, 46, 47, 48, 49]
list.dropLast(20) -> [1, 2, 3, 4, 5, 6, 7, 8, 9, 10,
 11, 12, 13, 14, 15, 16, 17, 18, 19, 20, 21, 22, 23,
 24, 25, 26, 27, 28, 29]

Process finished with exit code 0
```

The take functions

The `take` functions work in exactly the reverse way as the `drop` functions. You can take a group of elements from a collection and ignore the rest.

The following is an example:

```
fun main() {
    val list = IntArray(100) { it -> it * 10 }
    println("list.take(10) -> ${list.take(10)}") //(1)
    println("list.takeLast(10) -> ${list.takeLast(10)}") //(2)
    println("list.takeWhile { it <= 50 } -> ${list.takeWhile { it <= 50
}}") //(3)
    println("list.takeLastWhile { it >= 900 } -> ${list.takeLastWhile { it
>= 900 }}") //(4)
}
```

While the statement on comment (1) takes and prints the first 10 items from the array, the statement on comment (2) takes and prints the last 10 items from the array.

The statement on comment (3) is a bit different. Here, we used the `takeWhile` function. The `takeWhile` function takes a predicate and keeps taking items on the resultant collection while the predicate returns `true`. Once the predicate returns `false`, the `takeWhile` will stop checking for any more items and will return the resultant collection.

The `takeLastWhile` works in a similar way but from the reverse.

The following is the output:

```
list.take(10) -> [0, 10, 20, 30, 40, 50, 60, 70, 80, 90]
list.takeLast(10) -> [900, 910, 920, 930, 940, 950, 960, 970, 980, 990]
list.takeWhile { it <= 50 } -> [0, 10, 20, 30, 40, 50]
list.takeLastWhile { it >= 900 } -> [900, 910, 920, 930, 940, 950, 960,
970, 980, 990]
```

The zip function

The `zip` function does exactly what it sounds like. It zips collections. Confusing? Let's have a look at the following example:

```
fun main(args: Array<String>) {
    val names = listOf("Chandra", "Rivu", "Nick", "Ahmed")
    val ages = listOf(30, 27, 35, 19)
    println(names.zip(ages))
}
```

So, here we've created two `List` instances, the first one containing a few names (type is `String`), while the other `List` instance contains `Int`, representing their corresponding age. We then created a resultant list by zipping the `String` list with the `Int` list and printed the resultant list.

So, what will be the contents in the `resultantList`? How does the `zip` function operate?

Let's find out ourselves by going through the following output:

```
[(Chandra, 30), (Rivu, 27), (Nick, 35), (Ahmed, 19)]
```

Fantastic isn't it? The `zip` function takes each items by order from both the source collection and the collection provided in the argument, and returns a resultant collection containing pairs of those items.

 The `zip` operator only zips those items of the source collection, for which it could find a pair in the collection provided in the argument and ignores all the remaining source collection items from the resultant list.

Summary

So, in this chapter, we learned about collections and how to use them, or rather, how to utilize the collection objects rather than creating own data structures. We learned that there are two types of collections, namely mutable collections and immutable collections, and we learned to use them. We learned about the various collection types, including lists, maps and sets. We also learned about various data operations on collections. We started the chapter by exploring the collections framework in Kotlin and the data structure of collections. We gradually moved toward learning the data operations and functions that the Kotlin collections framework provides out of the box.

In `Chapter 9`, *Introduction to Functional Programming*, we will learn about functional programming, and how to implement it with the Kotlin language. We will also get introduced to the new functional library/companion of Kotlin; that is, the *Arrow* library.

Questions

1. Create a list of users and sort them by the following:
    *   Their ID
    *   Their name
    *   Their date of birth

2. Create a list of employees and filter out those whose salary is less than $800.

3. Let's assume a queue is there to buy movie tickets. Write a snippet that gives a ticket until the theater is house full. Assume the theatre has 200 seats.

4. Create a list of only prime numbers between 1 to 100.

9
Introduction to Functional Programming

In this chapter, you will learn about another programming paradigm, called **functional programming** (**FP**), and the data structures associated with it.

Up until this chapter, you've learned about various data structures and collections frameworks. This book is about data structures and algorithms, so why a chapter on functional programming? The reason is quite simple; although Kotlin is not a pure functional language, it provides out-of-the-box support for functional programming, and functional programming requires a number of new data structures. We want you to be familiar with them, as well.

In this chapter, we will cover the following topics:

- Introducing functional programming
- Immutability
- Exploring pure functions and their side effects
- Lambda and higher-order functions
- Functional data structures
- Introducing category theory

Introducing functional programming

Functional programming is a programming paradigm, just like **object-oriented programming** (OOP) or procedural programming. The definition of functional programming says, *functional programming is a programming system that relies on structuring the program as the evaluation of mathematical functions with immutable data, and it avoids state-change.*

Just as OOP requires you to model your program like real-life objects (such as trees, birds, and so on), functional programming requires you to distribute your program into small pieces of code, making it modular and non-complex. Just like OOP, functional programming encourages code reusability and abstraction. In many functional programming experts' opinions, functional programming is a more efficient evolution of OOP. So, it's better to consider functional programming not as contradictory to OOP, but as a more efficient version of OOP.

So, can we implement functional programming in any programming language? The answer is both yes and no. Just as with OOP, functional programming requires a few interfaces and support from the language; however, you can still follow the basic theories of functional programming in any language.

Immutability

In today's world, we cannot think of any application without concurrency. From network requests, to database/file access, to performing some calculations/computations in the background, concurrency is everywhere.

When dealing with concurrency, we need to make sure that our programs are thread-safe. Immutability is a great help, in that regard.

By default, functional codes are thread-safe, as they encourage immutability. So, what is immutability? If you go by the dictionary, when something is immutable, it is unchangeable; in programming, it refers to a variable that will always hold the same value after initialization. Thus, if the variable's value is not changing, it's automatically thread-safe.

Implementing immutability in Kotlin

Unlike other functional languages (such as Clojure, Haskell, F#, and so on), Kotlin doesn't enforce immutability; rather, it encourages immutability, giving automatic preference to immutability wherever possible.

In other words, Kotlin supports immutable variables (val), but no language mechanisms that would guarantee the true, deep immutability of the state. If a val references a mutable object, its contents can still be modified. Moreover, there's no guarantee that a val variable will always return the same value. It's true that a val variable cannot be modified, but with the help of a custom getter, you can return different values from a val variable.

To be more straightforward, Kotlin leaves the choice to the developer, and supports immutability if the developer wishes to use it.

For example, consider the following program:

```
val immutableRandomValue: String by lazy {
    getRandomValue()
}
fun getRandomValue(): String {
    val rand = Random().nextInt()
    return "Value $rand"
}

fun main(vararg args:String) {
    println("getRandomValue() will return different values at each call")
    println("1. ${getRandomValue()}")
    println("2. ${getRandomValue()}")
    println("\nHowever, immutableRandomValue will return the same value at
each call")
    println("1. $immutableRandomValue")
    println("2. $immutableRandomValue")
}
```

In the first three lines, we declared a variable, immutableRandomValue, with a val and with a lazy delegate. The lazy delegate allows you to initialize a variable in a lazy manner when it's first used, but once it's initialized, it always returns the same value, and never calls the block again.

Immutable collections

Along with the `val` datatype and `lazy` delegation, Kotlin also supports immutable collections, to enable developers to achieve more immutability. By default, any collection object is immutable.

Consider the following program from Chapter 8, *Collections and Data Operations in Kotlin*:

```
fun main(args: Array<String>) {
    val employeeList = listOf(
            Employee(2, "Chandra Sekhar Nayak"),
            Employee(1, "Rivu Chakraborty"),
            Employee(4, "Indranil Dutta"),
            Employee(3, "Sonkho Deep Mondal"),
            Employee(6, "Debraj Dey"),
            Employee(5, "Koushik Mridha")
    )

    employeeList.sortedBy {
        it.employeeID
    }.forEach {
        println(it)
    }
}
```

In this program, the `employeeList` is truly immutable; it's a `val` variable that holds an immutable list. When we are calling the `sortedBy` function on `employeeList`, it doesn't modify the `employeeList` itself; rather, it returns a new list that is sorted according to our algorithm (the `lambda` that we passed).

Exploring pure functions

When a function always returns the same value for a given parameter or parameter set and never modifies anything outside of the function scope (side effects), that function is called a **pure function**; in fact, you can replace no-argument pure functions with constants. The concept of a pure function is completely based on mathematical functions, for instance, in the mathematical function $y = f(x)$, for a given value of x, y (both constants).

Let's take a look at the following example:

```
class Calculator {
    var anyVariable: Int = 0

    fun add(a: Int, b: Int): Int = a + b        // pure function
```

```
fun multiply(a: Int, b: Int): Int = a * b      // pure function
fun subtract(a: Int, b: Int): Int = a - b      // pure function
fun divide(a: Int, b: Int): Int = a / b        // pure function

fun anyFunction(x: Int): Int {                 // not a pure function
    anyVariable = x + 2
    return anyVariable
}
}
```

The functions add, multiply, subtract, and divide are pure functions, since their return values for a given parameter set are constant, and they don't have any side effects. However, the anyFunction is not a pure function, even though its return value for a given parameter is constant, since it does have side effects.

 If a function modifies anything outside its own scope, then this behavior is called a **side effect**. For example, the value setters in OOP models and POJO classes contain side effects, since they modify the class-level variables and state, which are not inside the function.

Lambda and higher-order functions

In programming, a lambda, or lambda expression, generally refers to anonymous functions (functions without names or declarations). In Kotlin, a lambda expression starts with { and ends with }. It is called the **anonymous function/lambda expression**, since it doesn't contain a formal function declaration/name, but, rather, uses something more like a variable, containing an expression for a computation. Note that every lambda is a function, but every function might not be a lambda.

Lambda is strictly a language feature that isn't supported by all languages; for instance, Java didn't have support for lambda expressions till Java 8 came out, and till then, it only supported anonymous objects (instances of classes) for lambda, and not anonymous functions; in other words, you first had to create an interface, and only then could you pass that interface object as an anonymous class, like a lambda expression. However, as Kotlin treats functions its as first-class citizens, it has extensive support for lambda functions.

Now, what does it mean to treat functions as first-class citizens? In Kotlin, you can assign a function (lambda) to a variable, you can pass a function as a parameter from one function to another, and you can even nest functions inside of one another.

Let's look at an example to understand this:

```
fun main() {
    var myFunc: (Int) -> Int
    myFunc = { it * 2 }
    println("10 * 2 ${ myFunc(10) }")
    myFunc = { it / 2 }
    println("10 / 2 ${ myFunc(10) }")
}
```

In this example, we created a variable (`var`), `myFunc`, and then we assigned a function (`lambda`) to it and executed; we assigned another function, and executed the same. Quite interesting, isn't it?

Higher-order functions

So, you have learned what a `lambda` is; a higher-order function is simply a function that can take another function (read, `lambda`) as an argument or return another function (`lambda`). The following is an example:

```
fun highOrder(anotherFunc: () -> Unit) {
    println("Before anotherFunc()")
    anotherFunc()
    println("After anotherFunc()")
}
fun main() {
    highOrder {
        println("anotherFunc()")
    }
}
```

The function `highOrder` is a higher-order function; it expects `lambda`, which has no arguments, and returns `Unit` as its parameter. In Kotlin, if a higher-order function has only one parameter, and that's `lambda`, we can skip the parentheses; that's what we did while calling the `highOrder` function inside the main one.

Reading this (especially if you're new to functional programming), you'll probably be thinking—*Why on earth we would need to pass a function to another one, or return a function from another one?* Let's discuss a few possible scenarios for that. You may have used a lot of callbacks, or at least have heard of doing so, and it is a hell of a headache creating interfaces, then adding them as arguments to functions, passing them as anonymous objects, and then calling them from inside that function when a decided event occurs or a particular task is completed.

Extensive use of these callbacks leads to `callback` hell. Higher-order functions can save us from that.

For the simplest instance, think of a single-function `callback` interface (that is, a `callback` interface that contains only a single function); instead of using that, you can easily use a higher-order function and make the program a lot simpler. Let's try to understand this with an example:

```
interface ACallBack{
    fun someCallBackFunction()
}
fun listenToSomeEvent(callback: ACallBack) {
 // Event occurred
    callback.someCallBackFunction()
}
fun listenToSomeEvent(lambda: () -> Unit) {
 // Event Occurred
    lambda()
}
fun main() {
 // Using callback
    listenToSomeEvent(object: ACallBack {
    override fun someCallBackFunction() {
    println("Event occurred")
 }
 })

 // Using Lambda
    listenToSomeEvent {
    println("Event occurred")
 }
}
```

So, in this example, we tried to simulate the event listener code that we often write in our day-to-day life. We first created an event listener `callback`, then created a function that would accept an instance of that `callback` as the parameter, and would call the `callback` function when the event occurred. Then, in the `main` function, we called the function with an anonymous instance of that `callback`.

On the other hand, we also implemented the same functionality with a higher-order function, for which we just needed to create a higher-order function that would accept `lambda` as the parameter, and would call that when the event happened.

Doesn't the implementation with the higher-order function look more compact and straightforward than the `callback` one? That's the benefit of higher-order functions.

Functional data structures

In functional programming, there are a few unique data types and classes. We will discuss them here. Apart from the regular data types, functional programming allows you to have three different kinds of data types, listed as follows:

- **Type constructor**: This is a theoretical concept; please don't expect a constructor building a type. Even though type constructors are in FP, they are widely used even outside FP, under a different name—generic types. So, when a data type takes another type as a parameter, then that type is called a **type constructor**. The following are a few examples of type constructors:
  - List<T> (In Kotlin collections)
  - Map<K,T> (In Kotlin collections)
  - Option<T> (In ArrowKT)
  - Either<L,R> (In ArrowKT)

- **Type classes**: These are basically interfaces that allow you to define a set of extension functions over type constructors. These interfaces are mostly generic, and are expected to be implemented by any class that wants to support those sets of extension functions.

  For example, a functor (functors will be discussed later in this chapter) is a type class that defines the extension function map; the type constructors, such as Option, Either, and so on, implement the Functor interface to support the functor map.

- **Higher-kinded types**: These are basically type-level higher-order functions, such as functors or monads. To explain, let's first try to refresh your memory on what a higher-order function is. A high-order function is a function that takes another function as a parameter or returns a function, or both. So, basically, a higher-order function takes another function (lambda) as a parameter and transforms it into data or another function, or vice versa.

Similarly, higher-kinded types convert type constructors with type class constraints.

Understanding the Arrow framework and typed FP

As we are moving toward typed functional programming by learning about type constructors, type classes, and higher-kinded types, let's introduce Arrow, the functional companion to Kotlin's standard library. Kotlin, as a language, supports FP, and provides us with the required interfaces and language features to use FP in Kotlin; however, since Kotlin doesn't want to force FP and wants to leave the choice of which paradigm to use (that is, functional programming, OOP, or procedural) to the developer, it had to trade-off built-in typed FP.

Now, what is typed functional programming? Let's put it in the simplest terms. You can still use FP without using HK types, functors, monads, or applicatives (functors, monads, and applicatives will be explained later in this chapter), and, as we said earlier, even if you don't use these types, it will still be functional programming. However, using these types has its own benefits; they allow you to write your programs in a more pragmatic manner. Typed FP, sometimes referred to as pure FP, is a more pragmatic version of functional programming, which allows you to use these types and abstractions—HK types, functors, monads, or applicatives.

So, what do we mean when we say that the Kotlin standard library doesn't support built-in typed FP? Can't we use typed FP with Kotlin? The answer is yes; we can still use typed FP in Kotlin, by creating our own framework of typed FP, using the existing features of the Kotlin standard library, such as `sealed class`, `data class`, and so on. However, creating a framework for FP would be a tedious job, and would require us to deviate from the main objectives of our programs. It would also decrease the code readability, since new folks in the team might not understand the created framework, even if they have a good knowledge of FP.

The Arrow framework brings a solution to this problem; it's an open source framework that was created by a group of FP enthusiasts, designed to add typed FP support in Kotlin.

Now, let's start by adding Arrow to our project. The setup instructions are clearly written in the documentation at `https://arrow-kt.io/docs/#basic-setup`. For our project, we will be using Arrow version 0.8.2, the latest stale version at the time of writing this book.

The Arrow framework is quite a vast framework, with a lot of work from different people and a lot of support typed FP and pure FP. Covering all of the Arrow framework in one chapter would not be possible. We will be covering a basic introduction to the Arrow framework, along with a basic setup and examples of a couple of type constructors (`Option` and `Either`). To learn more about Arrow, please refer to the *Further reading* section of this chapter.

The Option type constructor

`Option` is a type constructor that allows you to define that a variable may or may not contain a value (in other words, the variable might be empty). If you're familiar with the Rx framework, you'll find this type constructor to be similar to `Maybe`; however, `Option` is more pragmatic and less like a stream.

The following is an example of the `Option` type constructor:

```
fun main() {
    var optionalVar: Option<Int>
    optionalVar = Some(10)
    println(optionalVar)
    optionalVar = None
    println(optionalVar)
}
```

You can assign a value to the `Option` variable, or you can assign `None`. The following is the output:

```
/Library/Java/JavaVirtualMachines/jdk1.8.0_181.jdk/Contents/Home/bin/java ...
Some(10)
None

Process finished with exit code 0
```

Now, you might be wondering—*Since Kotlin provides support for nullable types, what is the benefit of the* `Option` *type constructor?*

The following example might help you to understand one of its many benefits:

```
fun main() {
    printOptionalInt(Some(10))
    printOptionalInt(Some(2))
    printOptionalInt(None)
    printOptionalInt(Some(200))
```

```
        printOptionalInt(None)
    }

fun printOptionalInt(optionalInt: Option<Int>) {
    if(optionalInt is None) {
        println("It's blank")
    } else {
        println("It's ${optionalInt.getOrElse { 0 }}")
    }
}
```

The output for the preceding code is as follows:

```
/Library/Java/JavaVirtualMachines/jdk1.8.0_181.jdk/Contents/Home/bin/java ...
It's 10
It's 2
It's blank
It's 200
It's blank

Process finished with exit code 0
```

Although you can achieve the same functionality with a nullable type, Option allows you to write more pragmatic and easy-to-read programs.

Another benefit of using type constructors is the option to use the functors or monads associated with them.

The Either type constructor

The Either type constructor is unique. It allows you to define a variable that can hold two types of data, but one at a time. This is exceptionally helpful when you're making REST calls, so they can hold either an Exception instance (for failure) or the Response object (for success).

The following is a basic example of the Either type constructor:

```
fun main() {
    printResponse(fetchAPIData(Some(10)))
    printResponse(fetchAPIData(None))

}

fun fetchAPIData(someParameter: Option<Int>) : Either<Exception, String> {
    if(someParameter is None) {
        return Either.left(Exception("No value passed"))
```

```
        } else {
            return Either.right("The value is ${someParameter.getOrElse { 0
}}")
        }
    }

    fun printResponse(response : Either<Exception, String>) {
        println(if(response.isRight()) "Success $response" else "Failure
$response")
    }
```

So, in this program, we created a function that takes an `Option` and returns either `Exception` or `String`, based on the passed option. If the passed parameter is `None`, then the function will return `Exception`, or it'll return `String`. Achieving this functionality isn't quite possible without the `Either` type.

The output is as follows:

```
/Library/Java/JavaVirtualMachines/jdk1.8.0_181.jdk/Contents/Home/bin/java ...
Success Right(b=The value is 10)
Failure Left(a=java.lang.Exception: No value passed)

Process finished with exit code 0
```

Introducing category theory

Category theory is basically a mathematical discipline; if you're from a mathematics background (specifically, if you're a mathematician), then you probably know what we are going to present. Category theory has a wide range of applications in theoretical computer science and in functional programming. So, first, let's provide an overview and the basic concepts of category theory.

Mathematics itself is a stream; it has many branches (or categories), such as algebra, geometry, topology, analysis, probability, logic, and so on. It is evident that these different branches of mathematics share a few common structures/patterns/trends. It becomes exceptionally useful when you have a problem in a branch and you want help from a different branch. For example, you might have a problem in geometry, and by transporting it to algebra (a different branch), you'll be able to see the problem in a different light, and may discover new approaches and tools to solve the problem.

Seems cool, doesn't it? But for transporting a problem from one branch to another, you need a tool, something like a bridge. Category theory provides you with that bridge. Category theory identifies each branch explicitly; each branch has objects in it (for example, algebra has functions, set theory has sets, graph theory has graphs, group theory has groups, topology has topological spaces, and so on), and these objects can relate to one another in a sensible way (for example, sets relate via functions, groups relate via homomorphisms, topological spaces relate via continuous functions, and so on).

So, we can say that a category is a collection of objects that can relate to one another, via morphisms, in sensible ways, such as composition and associativity.

Category theory only deals with the relationship; it doesn't care what the elements of your set are, or whether your group is solvable, or whether your topological space has countable basics. It strips away a lot of detail from the objects, and the advantage of doing so is that your attention is diverted from the actual objects to the relationships among them.

We will not go further into the details of category theory, as this book mainly targets programming and not mathematics; however, you can read about it online. Trust me—the more you read about it, the more interesting you'll find it. Now, let's discuss how it is related to programming.

Functional programming is closer to math than any other paradigm; it models over mathematical objects, and the composition in category theory has a strong connection to programming. Composition is at the very heart of category theory; it's a part of the definition of the category itself, and we can easily say that composition is a programming essence. We programmers are always composing things. Structured programming is about making blocks of code composable. OOP is all about composing objects and their relationships. FP is not only about composing functions and algebraic data structures, but about composing concurrency, as well (in Kotlin, we can do that with coroutines). It's category theory from which the concepts of functors came, and from functors emerged the concepts of applicatives and monads.

So, what are we waiting for? Let's get started with functors, applicatives, and monads.

Functors

In category theory, a functor is a transformation between two categories. For example, suppose that `a` and `b` are two categories; the functor for `a` and `b` can then be written as `f(a):a->b`. This functor denotes that every object in the `a` category will be distinctly mapped (transformed) to the `b` category.

To explain this as a programmer, a functor will take a type constructor and will transform the item(s) within that type constructor.

For instance, suppose that you have a `List` of `Int`, `intList`, and you've created a function that will take this `intList` and will transform each item of the `List` into a `String` (and might do some additional modification, as well), and will return a `List` of `String` types.

The following is the programmatic interpretation of the preceding instance:

```
fun List<Int>.convertToStr(): List<String> =
    if (size > 0) {
        val newList = ArrayList<String>(size)
        for (item in this) {
            newList.add("Modified $item")
        }
        newList
    } else {
        emptyList()
    }


fun main(args: Array<String>) {
    val intList = listOf(1, 2, 3, 4, 5)
    println(intList.convertToStr())
}
```

So, in the preceding program, we have created an extension function on `List<Int>` that will convert our `intList` to a `List<String>`, appending each item with `"Modified "`.

The following is the output of the program:

```
/Library/Java/JavaVirtualMachines/jdk1.8.0_181.jdk/Contents/Home/bin/java ...
[Modified 1, Modified 2, Modified 3, Modified 4, Modified 5]

Process finished with exit code 0
```

Our `convertToStr` function can be called a functor, since it takes a type constructor (it's an extension function over `List<Int>`, which is essentially a type constructor over the `Int` data type), and transforms its values. You can also pass a `lambda`, to have better control over how to transform the items. Also, it's not necessary that a functor always changes the base data type of a type constructor. The definition of a functor says that it'll transform the type constructor. It may even transform the values of the items, as well; as long as it transforms a type constructor, it's a functor.

In the following example, we've used the Kotlin collections extension function, map, which is a typical example of functor:

```
fun main() {
    val intList = listOf(1, 2, 3, 4, 5)
    println(intList.map { it * 2 })
    println(intList.map { "Mapped $it" })
    println(intList.map { it.toDouble() })
}
```

Here, we used map to transform the list in various ways, with lambda. To learn more about the map function in Kotlin collections, please refer to Chapter 8, *Collections and Data Operations in Kotlin*.

The output of the preceding program is as follows:

```
/Library/Java/JavaVirtualMachines/jdk1.8.0_181.jdk/Contents/Home/bin/java ...
[2, 4, 6, 8, 10]
[Mapped 1, Mapped 2, Mapped 3, Mapped 4, Mapped 5]
[1.0, 2.0, 3.0, 4.0, 5.0]

Process finished with exit code 0
```

Arrow also supports the map functor; the following is an example of the map functor with Option:

```
fun main() {
    var optionalVal: Option<Int>
    optionalVal = Some(10)
    println(optionalVal.map { "It is $it" })
    optionalVal = None
    println(optionalVal.map { "It is $it" })
}
```

The output is as follows:

```
/Library/Java/JavaVirtualMachines/jdk1.8.0_181.jdk/Contents/Home/bin/java ...
Some(It is 10)
None

Process finished with exit code 0
```

Please note that the Option itself wasn't converted to String; rather, Some<Int> was transformed into Some<String>.

As a footnote, always remember that the main objective/functionality of a functor is that it allows you to transform the value(s) wrapped inside a single type constructor.

Applicatives

Applicatives are also called `applicative` functors, wherein a functor transforms a single type constructor. Applicative monads are capable of transforming multiple type constructors into a single one by taking them as input:

```
fun main() {
    val name: Option<String> = Some("Rivu")
    val company: Option<String> = Some("BYJUS")
    val city: Option<String> = Some("Bangalore")

    val authorInfo: Option<Tuple3<String, String, String>> =
        applicative<String, String, String, Tuple3<String, String,
String>>(name, company, city) { a, b, c ->
            Tuple3(a, b, c)
        }
    println("Author: $authorInfo")

}
```

In the preceding program, the `applicative` function is an `applicative` functor, since that function takes multiple type classes (here, three `Option` classes) as arguments, and transforms them into a single type class. We just call the `applicative` function with three options and a `lambda`, to process the values within the type classes.

The output of the preceding program is as follows:

```
/Library/Java/JavaVirtualMachines/jdk1.8.0_181.jdk/Contents/Home/bin/java ...
Author: Some(Tuple3(a=Rivu, b=BYJUS, c=Bangalore))

Process finished with exit code 0
```

The definition of the `applicative` function is as follows:

```
fun <A, B, C, R> applicative(
    optiona: Option<A>,
    optionb: Option<B>,
    optionc: Option<C>,
    block: (A, B, C) -> R
): Option<R> {
    return Some(block(optiona.getOrElse { None as A },
        optionb.getOrElse { None as B },
        optionc.getOrElse { None as C }
    ))
}
```

The function is simple; it just calls the block and returns an `Option` created from the value returned by the block.

Also, if we check the `lambda` function signature, we can see that the `lambda` function that the `applicative` requires is also a generic one; or, we can call it a wrapped function. In other words, an `applicative` functor applies a wrapped function to wrapped values, whereas a functor applies functions to wrapped values.

 A function that transforms a single type class is called a functor. If a function takes a single type class as a parameter (extension function, actually take the instance as parameter, upon which it's called) and returns an instance of the same type class (the wrapped type may be different or the same) with transformed values, it is called a `functor`. If a functor takes more than one type class as a parameter, then that functor is called an `applicative` functor. Therefore, you might say that all applicatives are functors, but not all functors are applicatives.

Monads

Monads are one of the most famous concepts in typed functional programming. Any content on typed FP that doesn't address monads is considered incomplete. A `monad` is also essentially a functor; the difference is that monads apply a function to a type constructor, where the function itself returns a type constructor. Does this sound confusing? Let's put it in a more simplistic way.

A functor applies a function to a type constructor to transform its values; the catch is that a particular function is deemed to return a raw value, and even if it returns another typed class, it is treated as a raw value. The same goes for applicatives.

So that you can better understand this, let's revisit our functor example with `map`, as follows:

```
fun main() {
    var optionalVal: Option<Int>
    optionalVal = Some(10)
    println(optionalVal.map { it+1 })//1
    println(optionalVal.map { Some(it+1) })//2
}
```

Before scrutinizing the program, let's take a look at the output:

```
/Library/Java/JavaVirtualMachines/jdk1.8.0_181.jdk/Contents/Home/bin/java ...
Some(11)
Some(Some(11))

Process finished with exit code 0
```

In the output, we can see that the first `map` (comment 1) returned `Some(11)`, an `Option` that contains the updated raw value `11`; but the second `map` (comment 2) returned `Some(Some(11))`, an `Option` that contains another `Option`, which has the raw value. Why? Let's find it.

So, on comment 2, from the `lambda` inside `map`, instead of returning a raw value, such as `Int` (as we did in comment 1) or `String`, we are returning another instance of `Option`. The `map`, being a simple functor, considers the returned `Option` as a raw value itself, and, finally, it returns a fresh instance of `Option` by putting the returned `Option` in it.

Monads are here to help you, in this case. Monads expect the function to only return a type constructor, and then flatten the returned type constructor before putting it in its final return type constructor.

The most common example of a `monad` functor is the `flatMap`. It's named `flatMap` since its entire functionality is similar to the `map` functor, except for the flattening part. So, let's look at an example to understand this:

```
fun main() {
    var someValue: Option<Int> = Some(10)
    println(someValue.flatMap { Some(it + 5) })
}
```

The output is as follows:

```
/Library/Java/JavaVirtualMachines/jdk1.8.0_181.jdk/Contents/Home/bin/java ...
Some(15)

Process finished with exit code 0
```

As we expected, the behavior of `flatMap` (and thus, the `monad`) is exactly similar to `map` (and thus, the functor), except that for the `monad`, we require the function (or `lamda`) to return a type constructor instead of a raw value, whereas for a functor, we expect the function (or `lambda`) to return a raw value.

These are the fundamental concepts of category theory, from mathematics to programming. These three data types (functors, applicatives, and monads), inspired by category theory, help to write functional programs in a more pragmatic and human-readable approach, while staying a few steps closer to mathematics.

Summary

In this chapter, you learned about functional programming and data structures, and the terminology associated with them. We started the chapter by covering the basic concepts associated with functional programming, such as pure functions, immutability, and so on. We then gradually moved towards typed FP, or pure FP, and covered the basics of the Arrow framework. Finally, you learned details about functor, `applicative`, and `monad`, after a short introduction to category theory and why it is important.

Further reading

- *Functional Kotlin*: https://www.packtpub.com/application-development/functional-kotlin
- Official Arrow documentation: https://arrow-kt.io/docs/
- *A Programmer's Introduction to Mathematics*: https://pimbook.org/

Other Books You May Enjoy

If you enjoyed this book, you may be interested in these other books by Packt:

Hands-On Object-Oriented Programming with Kotlin
Abid Khan, Igor Kucherenko

ISBN: 9781789617726

- Get an overview of the Kotlin programming language
- Discover Object-oriented programming techniques in Kotlin
- Understand Object-oriented design patterns
- Uncover multithreading by Kotlin way
- Understand about arrays and collections
- Understand the importance of object-oriented design patterns
- Understand about exception handling and testing in OOP with Kotlin

Learning Concurrency in Kotlin
Miguel Angel Castiblanco Torres

ISBN: 9781788627160

- Understand Kotlin's approach to concurrency
- Implement sequential and asynchronous suspending functions
- Create suspending data sources that are resumed on demand
- Explore the best practices for error handling
- Use channels to communicate between coroutines
- Uncover how coroutines work under the hood

Leave a review - let other readers know what you think

Please share your thoughts on this book with others by leaving a review on the site that you bought it from. If you purchased the book from Amazon, please leave us an honest review on this book's Amazon page. This is vital so that other potential readers can see and use your unbiased opinion to make purchasing decisions, we can understand what our customers think about our products, and our authors can see your feedback on the title that they have worked with Packt to create. It will only take a few minutes of your time, but is valuable to other potential customers, our authors, and Packt. Thank you!

Assessments

The GitHub URL for the answers of the Questions section of chapters is here:

```
https://github.com/PacktPublishing/Hands-On-Data-Structures-and-Algorithms-
with-Kotlin/tree/master/Assessments
```

Index

www.ingramcontent.com/pod-product-compliance
Lightning Source LLC
LaVergne TN
LVHW081524050326
832903LV00025B/1616

* 9 7 8 1 7 8 8 9 9 4 0 1 9 *